CALVIN S. BROWN

TONES
INTO WORDS

Musical Compositions
as Subjects of Poetry

The University of Georgia Press
Athens

Copyright 1953

THE UNIVERSITY OF GEORGIA PRESS

Library of Congress Catalog Card No. 53-11755

Printed in the United States of America

FOOTE & DAVIES, INC. Atlanta

TONES INTO WORDS

Contents

Preface

◇

This work presents in some detail a study of one of the types of musico-literary relationships which are discussed in my *Music and Literature: a Comparison of the Arts* (University of Georgia Press, Athens, 1948). The specific problem here treated — the use of individual musical compositions as subjects for poetry — can be seen in better perspective if approached with the background of this more general consideration of the relationships of music and literature. It has, however, seemed advisable to present this study in such a way that it can be read and understood independently. For this reason, some of the material treated in detail in the earlier work has been here summarized, and where this has been done the reader can find full discussions in *Music and Literature* if he desires more information than is necessary for the present purpose. For the sake of the reader who is already familiar with *Music and Literature,* repetition of material there presented has been held to a minimum, and when it has been necessary to cover the same ideas and problems, different illustrations have been used wherever this was feasible.

For the convenience of the reader, a separation has been effected between translations and explanations, which are designated by asterisks and printed as footnotes, and citations of the sources of material, which are given in the form of numbered notes at the back of the book.

The bibliographies are selected to suggest some of the most useful works for further reading. Consequently they omit some works actually cited in the notes, and include some which are not cited. They make no pretense at an exhaustive listing of the works in this field of study: my own bibliography of musico-literary relationships now contains about 2,200 items.

The list of individual poems on identifiable musical compositions, on the other hand, is as complete as I can make it, even to the point of including a few poems which I have been unable to examine. However, it also makes no claim to exhaustiveness. Because of the obscurity of many of the versifiers who have engaged

vii

in this type of writing and the necessarily haphazard methods of locating their efforts, a great many poems must inevitably have been overlooked.

It is impossible to express my indebtedness to all the friends who have given aid and comfort in this undertaking, both by calling new material to my attention and by their reception of my other studies in this general field. But I cannot close my introductory remarks without an expression of gratitude to my wife, whose help has run the whole gamut from inspiration — which is necessary for the production of even uninspired works — to typing.

CALVIN S. BROWN

Athens, Georgia

Acknowledgements

⬦

The author wishes to express his indebtedness to the following persons and publishers for permission to quote material on which they hold copyrights:

Mr. Conrad Aiken and the Oxford University Press for passages from the poetry and criticism of Conrad Aiken; George Allen & Unwin, Ltd., for material from John Todhunter's *Sounds and Sweet Airs;* Constable & Co., Ltd., for the sonnet from Mary Alice Vialls' *Music Fancies and Other Verses;* E. P. Dutton, Inc., N. Y., for passages from Vernon Lee's *Music and its Lovers;* Harper & Brothers for Edna Millay's "On Hearing a Symphony of Beethoven," from *The Buck in the Snow and Other Poems,* published by Harper & Brothers, Copyright, 1928, by Edna St. Vincent Millay; Houghton Mifflin Co. for passages from *The Poems of Celia Thaxter* and from Richard Watson Gilder's *A Book of Music* and *The Fire Divine;* the estate of Edgar Lee Masters and The Macmillan Co. for passages from Masters' "Beethoven's Ninth Symphony and the King Cobra," from *Invisible Landscapes;* The Oxford University Press, Inc., for material from Sir George Grove's *Beethoven and his Nine Symphonies;* the estate of Henry Aylett Sampson, for passages from his *Sonnets and Other Poems;* Mr. Percy Scholes for a passage from his *Crotchets: a Few Short Musical Notes;* Charles Scribner's Sons for a passage from *The Poems of Alice Meynell;* and The Viking Press for two passages from Siegfried Sassoon's *Satirical Poems.*

The author also wishes to extend his thanks to the University of Georgia for a grant which made the publication of this study possible.

CHAPTER I

A Survey of Musical Literature

The relations between music and poetry have been the subject of many studies in literary history and aesthetics, but, broadly speaking, we may reduce the possible relationships to five general classes. Music may be a constant companion of poetry, so that neither art is complete without the other, as was probably the case with primitive song. It may have no relation whatsoever to poetry, each of the two arts going quietly on its own way, to all appearances ignorant of the other's existence. Between these two extremes we may find poetry trying to imitate music by using various elements of poetic art to create the effects of similar elements in music, and poetry of this type actually seeks to replace music. The fourth possibility is that poetry, without having a musical accompaniment or seeking to reproduce the sound effects of music, may take music as its subject and proceed to describe, analyze, or interpret it by means of words. Finally, "program" music may, by attempting narration or description without verbal aid, seek to seize for itself the functions generally attributed to poetry.

The third and fourth of these relationships — the imitation of music and the description or interpretation of it — form the subject of the present study. However, music exists in so many varieties that it is practically impossible to know what an author has in mind unless he refers to some specific composition definitely enough to enable us to identify it. Hence we shall speak almost entirely of writings dealing with specific compositions. The discussion will be largely limited to works in verse, for in prose we find numerous vague uses of music as a part of the atmosphere or setting in novels; also, in prose we can draw no sharp dividing line between attempts at an artistic treatment of a piece of music and simple program notes, technical descriptions, or analyses.

This study, then, will deal with verse descriptions of musical compositions. It will attempt to show briefly the history of such attempts, then to study their varying techniques and methods of approach, and finally to evaluate them. Most of the poetry with which we shall be concerned is distinctly minor verse, and some of it is definitely bad, but it all has its value for our purposes. Every poem at least represents an author's serious attempt at expressing an idea, a sentiment, or a sensation, and in a study of the attempts to treat music poetically the failures are as instructive as the successes.

It is only within the last century that music has come to be extensively used as a subject for poetry and that poems on specific pieces of music have become at all common. It is interesting to note that the increase in such poems seems to have come primarily from general literary trends and to owe little to the influence of one poet on another. A brief outline of the history of music among the poets will serve to indicate some of the elements involved in attempts to treat music in verse, and will furnish a background for a more detailed discussion of individual problems.

The art of music is — in the opinion of poets, at least — a comparatively new one, and its early stages have little of interest for this study. Primitive poetry and music seem to have been inseparable. The minstrels of Homer always took up a harp or lyre before beginning their recitations, and the choral odes of Greek tragedy were certainly accompanied by instruments. It is probable that by the time of Horace, if not earlier, Rome had developed poetry that was to be read rather than sung, and poetry of this type has been in existence ever since that time, although lyric poetry remained generally true to its name for several centuries more. The fixed classical meters left little opportunity for imitating music, and since there was practically no music without words, the idea of describing it was not likely to be considered. Trying to interpret it was unheard of, for music necessarily meant what its words said. The only interpretations during the Middle Ages were symbolical, and dealt with the mysterious properties of numbers and intervals, or with the imaginative parallels that could be drawn between musical instruments and religious ideas. Thus St. Augustine compared cymbals to human lips,[1] and Honoré d'Autun

(c. 1120) wrote a very ingenious interpretation:

Psalterium . . . forma sua corpus Christi exprimit. Dum enim inferius percutitur, superius resonat . . . quod fit in triangulo psalterio hoc est in confessione Trinitatio, et in decem chordis, id est in decem praeceptis legis . . . Psalterium quod de superioribus sonat animam, cithara quod de inferioribus sonat, significat corpus. Per psalterium etiam contemplativa vita, per citharam exprimitur activa . . . Chordae sunt intestina animalia exsiccata et attenuata dulciter resonantia; et designant internas cogitationes justorum, vigiliis et jejuniis exsiccatas et meditationes attenuatas dulcissimum melos purae conscientiae resonantes.[2]

The psaltery . . . by its shape represents the body of Christ. For when it is struck from beneath, it resounds above. . . . The fact that the psaltery is made in the shape of a triangle is a confession of the Trinity, and the ten strings represent the Ten Commandments. . . . Since the psaltery sounds from above, it represents the soul; since the cither sounds from below, it represents the body. Also, the psaltery signifies the contemplative life, and the cither, the active life. . . . The strings are the intestines of animals, dried out and stretched so that they resound sweetly; and they signify the inward thoughts of the just, dried out by vigils and fasts, and stretched by meditation so that they resound with the ravishing music of a clean conscience.

Discussion of this sort has, of course, nothing to do with music.

During the next few centuries we find occasional mention of songs, but most writers show little interest in music. When Dante mentions the *Vexilla Regis Prodeunt*[3] he is concerned only with the words, which are parodied as "Vexilla regis prodeunt inferni," and, in spite of some occasional mention of the music, the text is similarly responsible for the mention of every hymn which he cites. Chaucer mentions several songs, but apparently without great attention to the music. A more technical interest is shown by Henryson, who has a passage[4] bristling with such forbidding mediaeval musical terms as Emetricus, Eneolus, Dyaterseron, and, among others, "Epodyus rycht hard and curious." However, after Henryson has described the music of the spheres in a few stanzas of such technicalities, he confesses:

> Off sik musik to wryte I do but dote,
> Tharfor at this mater a stra I lay,
> For in my lyf I coud nevir syng a note.

The habit of an ignorant use of musical terms in poetry began early!

It is a strange coincidence that perhaps the earliest piece of verse actually describing a musical composition deals with *Ut Queant Laxis*, which, since it gave the syllables of our present scale

their names, may be called the beginning of modern music. Lydgate's poem *Incipit de Musica*[5] describes Dame Musyk's teaching
of musical notation, harmony, melody, and instruments, and tells
us that

> She taught six syllables which we notes clepe
> And in her crafte they necessary bene
> Whiche on an ympore thou mayest brynge to kepe
> If thou his meter can proporcyon clene
> Ut queant laxis is it, which i mene
> There mayst thou find ut, re, my, fa, sol, la
> These syllables syxe used dame Musica.

Each line of this hymn began one degree of the scale higher than
the preceding line, and the syllables quoted are the respective first
syllables of the lines. Each syllable gave its name to the degree of
the scale on which it stood, and, with the substitution of *do* for *ut*
in some languages and the addition of *ti* for the leading-tone, this
scale is preserved today.

With the Renaissance the separation between lyric poetry and
music may be said to have begun, and the insistence of the poets
of the Pléiade that verse should be set to music and sung is evidence of this fact: it would never have occurred to a *trouvère* or a
Minnesinger to insist on anything so obvious. Ronsard mentions
music in several passages, particularly in connection with the performances of Cassandre, but he seems to have been interested in
music chiefly as a stimulant to love or an evoker of its memories.[6]
This attitude is common throughout French literature. Intimately
connected with the poets of the Pléiade was Paul Schede, who
imbibed their musical theories and returned to Germany to propa-
gate them. Under the name of Paul Melissus he wrote Latin poems,
a number of which were addressed to musicians. *Ad Orlandum
Lassum*[7] is one of the best of these, and parts of it go into some
detail as to the qualities of Orlando's music:

> Primus inexpertam scrutatus es impiger artem;
>   Te duce LASSE novum Musica tentat iter:
> Artis & ad summum divina peritia vênit,
>   Suaviter harmonicos te modulante sonos.
> Es gravis, & plenis aures concentibus imples,
>   Maiestasque tuis cantibus omnis inest.
> Scis bene, quae faciat laetas symphonia mentes,
>   Flebilibusque modis scis bene quâ sit opus.

You first diligently examined the untested art; under your leadership, Lassus,
music strikes out on a new path, and when you sweetly modulate the sounds

of harmony divine skill reaches the height of art. You are mighty, and fill our ears with full harmonies. All majesty is in your songs. You know well what music rejoices our hearts, and you know also the use of melancholy strains.

Melissus has at least eight poems to the composer Marcus Antonius Muretus.

While the effect of the Pléiade was still strong in France, and while Melissus was vainly trying to make it felt in Germany, England was coming independently to a wider use of music in poetry. Spenser has a remarkable stanza[8] describing the sirens' song:

> With that the rolling sea, resounding soft,
> In his big base them fitly answered;
> And on the rocks the waves breaking aloft
> A solemne Meane unto them measured;
> The whiles sweet zephyrus lowd whisteled
> His treble, a straunge kinde of harmony,
> Which Guyons senses softly tickeled,
> That he the boatman bad row easily,
> And let him heare some part of their rare melody.

Spenser's conception of this music of nature is quite clear: it is a four-part harmony, with the sea for bass, the splashing waves for tenor, the sirens for altos, and the wind for a treble. The altos have the melody, and the treble is singing a descant above it. In several other passages Spenser shows a similar interest in music and accuracy in its description.

In 1596, ten years after the publication of Melissus' works, Sir John Davies published *Orchestra, or A Poeme on Dauncing*. This work of nearly a thousand lines begins with Penelope's suitors' attempts to persuade her to dance, and her refusal. One of them tells her of the beauties and pleasures of the dance and finally persuades her. In the course of the argument he describes a number of standard dances, with some mention of their music, particularly from a rhythmical point of view.

During the Elizabethan period England was one of the most musical countries of Europe, and her leadership continued until about the end of the seventeenth century. There are many musical allusions in the literature of this period,* but few of them are very definite. Both Shakespeare[9] and Milton[10] are among the rare authors who speak of music intelligently, feelingly, and accurately;

---

*The custom of printing versified tributes to a composer by way of preface to a volume of his music is responsible for a considerable quantity of poetry. See Boyd, M. C., *Elizabethan Music and Musical Criticism* (Philadelphia, 1940), *passim*.

Shakespeare often mentions songs and ballads by name, and Milton's descriptions of organ music are among the finest in literature. Milton and Waller wrote complimentary poems to Henry Lawes, and other poets of their time dedicated verses to various composers and singers. However, from the poets' view music was still largely vocal, and we find little interest in the music for its own sake, except in passages such as Milton's description of the fugue[11] or of contrapuntal music in general,[12] and these refer to no specific compositions. The same thing may be said of Dryden's St. Cecilia's Day poems. From Dryden's day onward French classical influence was dominant in England and, in spite of Handel, music did not return to real prominence in literature until the nineteenth century.

As we have already remarked, the split between music and poetry was beginning in France at the time of Ronsard, and by the end of the seventeenth century it was well advanced. Music was used with various plays and operas, but few writers took it seriously. Generalizations on the spirit of any age are dangerous, but it is probable that the *bon sens* of French classicism was essentially opposed to an art which could not be explained or rationalized by the system of criticism in vogue for literature. At any rate, we find it mentioned more in connection with serenades in comic intrigues than in any other capacity.

Germany also separated verse and melody early in the seventeenth century, under the somewhat pedantic poetry of a late Renaissance. Weckherlin published his poems in 1616, and Calvin Thomas says of them that "the songs are purely literary productions, and mark the beginning of the modern dissociation of music and lyric poetry."[13] Opitz eight years later put the practice of Weckherlin into the form of literary dogma, and music declined. As the century progressed French influence became ever stronger until music practically vanished from the literary scene. Though the "Swiss painters" to a certain extent broke with their French models, since their field was landscape description they did not change the status of music. By the beginning of the eighteenth century classicism had almost completely removed music from the literature of France, Germany, and England.

The rise of instrumental music had its share in the temporary neglect of the art among men of letters. Since instrumental music did not aid their poetry, they could see no point in it. It could not be put into words, and words were their means of expression.

Even the musicians regarded it as a weak echo of song, and this view, prevalent in the time of Pope and Voltaire, is not unknown today. Charles Avison states that "the finest *instrumental Music* may be considered as an Imitation of the vocal."[14] In France, Grétry held the same theory, and defined instrumental music as "un discours de sons, le chant d'un discours dont on a retranché les paroles."[15] The opinion of literary men on musical matters is well shown by an epigram, attributed to both Pope and John Byrom, on the feuds between Handel and Bononcini:

Strange that such difference should be
'Twixt Tweedledum and Tweedledee.

And Fontenelle probably voiced the general opinion when, growing impatient at a performance of instrumental music, he exclaimed, "Sonate, que me veux-tu?"[16] Under such circumstances it was natural that musical poetry should not flourish, and the considerable number of epigrams[17] on composers and operas which this period produced are little more than clever ways of saying that the works are either superb or contemptible.

However, the rise of instrumental music into a position of prominence served to develop the musically inspired poem. The general public might disapprove, but those who were interested in music now had an opportunity to express themselves on it, for there was now no text which, being sung to the music, would naturally be considered as its meaning. An eighteenth century poem *On Handel's Performance on the Organ, and His Opera of Alcina*[18] had, like many others of the same period, little more than general praise, but its century produced two works which attempted to form a close association between instrumental music and lyric poetry.

The Italian violinist and composer, Antonio Vivaldi (c. 1680-1743), became a descriptive poet for his own music in his Opus 8, *Il cimento dell' armonia e dell' invenzione*. The first four numbers of this work are four concertos entitled *La Primavera, L'Estate, L'Autunno,* and *L'Inverno*. Each of these concertos is accompanied by a sonnet divided into lettered parts, and in the score each of these separate parts is printed above the passage in the music to which it applies. Thus the composer's own program is written out in a poetic form and very clearly correlated with his music.[19]

Later in the century the poet H. W. von Gerstenberg undertook to interpret a Fantasia of C. Ph. E. Bach. His work, which

appeared in C. F. Cramer's *Flora* (1787), consisted of two alterna-
tive vocal parts, both soliloquies, entitled *Hamlet* and *Socrates,* and
set to two different melodies, both of which were derived from
the right-hand part of the Fantasia.[20] This work is particularly interesting as an early admission of the inability of instrumental
music definitely to suggest a situation, or even a mood, for to
Gerstenberg the same composition could equally well suggest
Socrates calmly meeting death and Hamlet excitedly meditating
suicide.

The nineteenth century brought with it a greatly increased
musical interest among men of letters throughout Europe, and a
corresponding flow of musical literature. All the tendencies of the
period probably contributed to this sudden revival of sensibility.
The classicists had usually admitted that music was the language
of the emotions and of the soul, but they had not desired a language
which, according to their ideas, addressed their souls unreason-
ably. With the romantic emphasis on a full emotional life music
naturally came into prominence. The demand for individuality
also played its part, for music, as we shall see later, causes widely
different responses in different hearers. The shift of interest from
the universal to the particular made for more attention to actual
compositions by human composers and a corresponding decrease
in the proportion of musical literature devoted to the spheres and
heavenly choirs, although the fondness for the Aeolian harp in
romantic poetry shows that the taste for vague music and vaguer
rhapsody was far from dead.

It is interesting to note another possible explanation of the
musical tendencies of nineteenth-century literature. Mr. Flinders
Petrie has developed a remarkable theory of cycles of civilization,
according to which a cycle lasts from twelve hundred to two thousand years. Within each cycle the arts reach maturity in the same
order.[21] Mr. Cecil Gray has expanded this theory as it applies to
the most recent cycles (of which we naturally have the most detailed knowledge), and has pointed out that during the period of
maturity and perfection of any one art, all the others tend to
draw their inspiration from it, and even to imitate it. Thus Dante's
Commedia, written during the domination of architecture, is architectural both in its own structure and in many of its descriptions.[22] Since the nineteenth century is the period of musical maturity and dominance, it is only to be expected that the other arts
should be concerned with music, and since literature is the art

most closely related to music, its concern with music will naturally be more immediate and more extensive than that of, say, sculpture.

When writers and musicians had begun to part company instrumental music had been an experiment, but the poets of the nineteenth century returned to music because it was a mature art which had already produced works comparable with the greatest glories of literature. It was only to be expected that Germany, having developed this new art, would be the first to recognize and applaud it. It must be remembered, however, that there was a general change in attitude which cannot be satisfactorily expressed by the names of those few authors and works which can be mentioned here. Formerly a contented ignorance of musical matters had been the rule among poets; henceforth it was the exception.

There were many reasons for the romanticists' increased interest in music, and this interest itself was only a part of a larger tendency towards "the romantic confusions of the arts."[23] Since about 1800, writers had been trying by means of one art to secure the effects of another, and we find poems on paintings and music, paintings on music and poetry, musical compositions on poems and pictures — in fact, practically every possible combination of the arts. Along with these we find attempts at new arts employing the principles of music, but using color[24] and scent[25] for their materials, and there are literary descriptions of symphonies of liqueurs[26] and cheeses.[27] The extent of this mixture of the arts is easily shown by the fact that the pictures of Böcklin have inspired at least seven symphonic poems and one symphony, by five different composers.[28] In a period which fostered such close relationships between arts so different as painting and music we are not surprised to find the connections between music and poetry far closer than they have ever been before.

Tieck and the Schlegels did a service to music by their respect for it, but, in spite of Tieck's attempts at verbal music in the overture and entr'actes of *Die verkehrte Welt,* and the attempt at dealing with a specific work in his poem on Pergolesi's *Stabat Mater,*[29] it was left to Wackenroder and E. T. A. Hoffmann to make musical literature a reality.[30] Each of these writers invented a musician to be his spokesman in musical matters, and each contributed to the German metaphysical conception of music as a final synthesis of the universe. Wackenroder's ideas are revealed in the life of the fictitious musician, Joseph Berglinger, in the *Herzensergiessungen eines kunstliebenden Klosterbruders* (1797). Theoretically, Wackenroder condemned the practice of trying to interpret music by words, but the influence of such passages as the following cannot be doubted:

Bei fröhlichen und entzückenden vollstimmigen Symphonien, die er vorzüglich liebte, kam es ihm gar oftmals vor, als säh' er ein munteres Chor von Jünglingen und Mädchen auf einer heitern Wiese tanzen, wie sie vor- und rückwärts hüpften, und wie einzelne Paare zuweilen in Pantomimen zueinander sprachen, und sich dann wieder unter den frohen Haufen mischten. Manche Stellen in der Musik waren ihm so klar und eindringlich, dass die Töne ihm Worte zu sein schienen.[31]

When hearing joyous and delightful full-voiced symphonies, which he especially loved, he often felt as if he saw a cheerful chorus of youths and maidens dancing in a pleasant meadow, skipping forward and backward, with single pairs occasionally speaking to each other in pantomime and then mixing in with the joyous group again. Many passages in the music were so clear and impressive that the notes seemed to him to be words.

In subsequent musical literature we often meet this chorus, and we find that many authors have set down the words which the music seemed to say. *Ein wunderbares morgenländisches Märchen von einem nackten Heiligen*[32] gives allegorically the conception of music later developed to its fullest extent by Schopenhauer.

E. T. A. Hoffmann was a creative artist in literature, music, and painting, and was the most influential of the German romantic writers on music. In the *Fantasiestücke in Callots Manier* (variously dated 1813, 1814, and 1815), his musical mouthpiece, Johannes Kreisler, is introduced. He is a sound musician, but a fantastic character who often gives interpretations of music in terms of color, light, and motion. Of Mozart's *Symphony in E Flat Major* we are told that

Liebe und Wehmut tönen in holden Geisterstimmen; die Nacht geht auf in hellem Purpurschimmer, und in unaussprechlicher Sehnsucht ziehen wir nach den Gestalten, die, freundlich uns in ihre Reihen winkend, in ewigem Sphärentanze durch die Wolken fliegen.[33]

Love and melancholy sound in friendly spirit-voices; night comes on in a glow of crimson, and with ineffable longing we approach the forms which, beckoning invitingly to us, fly through the clouds in the eternal dance of the spheres.

Kreisler's musikalisch-poetischer Klub gives a monologue which Kreisler improvised at the piano, and tells us the accompaniment throughout in terms of chords and dynamics, with, of course, an implied correlation between the effect of the accompaniment and the meaning of the monologue. In spite of these fantastic performances, Hoffman was a good, sound musical critic when he wished to be: though Beethoven rather made a point of ignoring musical criticism, he wrote Hoffman a letter of thanks for being the only contemporary critic who really understood him.[34]

After Wackenroder and Hoffman we are not surprised to find the German literature of the nineteenth century full of music. Grillparzer, who was himself a good pianist and a student of musical theory,[35] wrote various poems and essays on music, as well as several verses on specific compositions.[36] Most of these, however, merely take the music as a point of departure, and deal with some other subject. *Klara Wieck und Beethoven* praises the virtuosa for her simple and perfect performance of the *F Minor* ("Appassionata") *Sonata; Zu Beethoven's Egmont-Musik* discusses the play more than the incidental music; and *Stabat Mater* attacks the public for failing to appreciate Rossini (and for tending to confuse the media of the arts). *Paganini* speaks of the violinist's self-revelation in his playing, in connection with a fantastic legend about his life. A poem written on the day of Beethoven's death describes his reception into heaven by the geniuses who had died before him. There is also an epigram on his *Ninth Symphony*. Less specific works include several poems to musicians (including Mozart, Liszt, and Meyerbeer) and a number of short verses dealing with musical aesthetics.

The general interest in music among the German poets of this century is shown by the fact that Zedlitz, Brentano, Lenau, Keller, Heyse, and Dahn also wrote poems to Beethoven, and Kopisch, Tieck, Liliencron, and Dehmel are among the many who wrote verses to other composers. Musical instruments are the subjects of poems by Schubart, Tieck, Fitger, and others, and there was a host of poems on Orpheus and Arion, on the Aeolian harp, and on the lives of imaginary composers. Prose literature was equally full of musical references of one kind or another. Throughout the century the interest remained at a consistently high level: Liliencron could be taken as a later counterpart of Grillparzer. However, about the beginning of the twentieth century Germany was to experience, along with France, England, and America, a still greater poetical interest in music, and to produce authors who habitually took specific compositions for their subjects.

The rise of musical literature in France in the nineteenth century has been well studied by Fernand Baldensperger in a volume entitled *Sensibilité musicale et romantisme*.[37] He finds that there was something of a revival of interest in music about 1784, when there were a number of concerts and criticisms of music, but he questions the sincerity of this interest. The Revolution did a good deal towards increasing musical interest and especially towards creating a tolerance for instrumental music, for the aristocrats in exile were forced to listen to songs without being able to understand the words. This experience naturally led to an interest in the song as music, and the influence of the period of exile is visible in the works of Xavier de Maistre, whose writings after his return show a far greater musical interest than did his earlier works. At first melody was the chief delight of the poets, but they later came to have some appreciation of harmony. Mme. de Staël used music frequently, especially in *Corinne,* where it was sometimes a sentimental ornament, and sometimes an essential part of the work. The younger generation of the Napoleonic era was inclined to see in music a liberator of the individual soul. Gérard de Nerval and Alfred de Vigny were among the most musically sensitive of this group, while Victor Hugo was, in spite of various flattering references to music, both indifferent and ignorant; "Hugo, ce n'est pas douteux, n'a jamais été en vive sympathie avec l'art du chant et de l'orchestre."[38]

George Sand had, by her intimacy with Chopin and Liszt, an unusual opportunity for hearing and understanding music, and her works frequently reflect her interest. One of them, *Le Contrebandier, paraphrase fantastique sur un rondo fantastique de Franz Liszt*[39] is an amazing example of the use of a theme and variations in literature, and succeeds remarkably well in suggesting the effect of music.

Music exerted some influence on poetic forms, and the application of musical terms to poetry became common. From 1818 to 1825 there was a steady increase in musical discussion, and in the latter year it was even common in the newspapers, but during 1829 and 1830 interest fell off again. The worship of the virtuoso, the general apathy of the public, and the departure of Fétis, who had done much for the musical education of France, all combined to produce a decline which Vigny and Stendhal lamented, but were powerless to stop.

From 1830 until about 1885 the separation of music and poetry was nearly complete. Occasional works contained musical references, but the French poets devoted themselves for the most part to painting and sculpture. When music appeared it was usually treated in a non-musical manner. Gautier is the supreme example. His *Variations sur le Carnaval de Venise*[40] reveal him as essentially visual in all his poetic imagery. It used to be said that the author of the celebrated *Symphonie en blanc majeur*[41] was essentially anti-musical, but this idea has been exploded. The definition of music as "the most disagreeable and expensive of all noises," on which the charge was largely based, was only quoted by Gautier, and we must remember that a *selected* edition of his musical criticisms runs to six volumes of competent, common-sense work, uninspired though it may be.[42] The falsity of some musical pretensions during this period is best shown by Laprade, who published a volume of poems entitled *Symphonies* (1855), and later wrote a polemic *Contre la musique* (1881). This latter work pretends to attack only the excesses and vices of music, but it manages to include practically all recognized music in its condemnation and to give the impression that Laprade hated bad music, but loved none.

Somewhat earlier Théodore de Banville had made what seemed superficially to be a stand for good music. In 1842 he began a violent attack on the Opéra. He continued this for several years, writing satirical pieces of all kinds, attacking the composers, and insulting the performers and audiences, but his own musical taste was little better than that which he attacked; it was merely different. "Il n'a pas de goût musical. Mais il a eu pour la musique cette belle foi qui fut si rare chez les lettrés de son temps."[43] His chief criterion seems to have been the taste of the general public, which was always to be condemned: "La haine du bourgeois, c'est elle, en fin de compte, qui entraine Banville dans cette croisade musicale."[44] His one poem worthy of serious consideration, from our point of view, is *La dernière pensée de Weber* (1845), which attempts to translate the musical impression into verse. A quotation from Hoffman introduces the poem, and shows whence Banville took the idea of such an attempt.

Cœuroy, in summarizing the differences between the musical interests of the Germans and the French, says that the Germans use all forms of music, especially instrumental sounds.

C'est là ce qui les distingue nettement des romantiques français. Ceux-ci n'ont jamais songé à subordonner à la musique les arts et la philosophie. Leur seul concession, c'est d'aimer la voix ou, plus précisément, la cantatrice, Ils considèrent la personne humaine. Les Allemands considèrent la sonorité; ils ne cessent de répéter que la musique occupe une place à part, qu'elle est mystérieuse parce qu'elle possède un élément obscur et indescriptible, le son.[45]

This fact clearly distinguishes them from the French romanticists. The latter never dreamed of subordinating philosophy or the other arts to music. Their only concession was to love the voice — or, more exactly, the woman who owned it. They thought of the person. The Germans thought of the sound: they never tired of repeating that music is unique and mysterious because it has the obscure and indescribable element of sound.

The distinction between loving the voice and loving the singer is important; French poetry is full of references to music which is loved because someone once performed it under some particular circumstances. We find that music is used merely as a setting for scenes or thoughts of love more frequently, on the whole, in French poetry than in English or German, although this use is common enough in all three.*

A revival of interest about 1885 made musical references in French literature both commoner and more intelligent. Wagner had his definite following, particularly in the novel,[46] and the influence of Baudelaire was noticeable. This growth in musical interest in France coincided with a similar development in England and, to a certain extent, in Germany, although the high level there throughout the nineteenth century prevented the movement's being so conspicuous as in the other countries.

English romanticism was not particularly musical, except in a somewhat vague, uninformed way. Few of the writers show any specific interest, or name any particular composers or works, and the antagonistic references to music are more striking than the favorable ones. Lamb attacked it in his *Chapter on Ears,* and broke the general silence in his *Free Thoughts on Several Eminent Composers,*[47] which begins

> Some cry up Haydn, some Mozart
> Just as the whim bites; for my part,
> I do not care a farthing candle
> For either of them, or for Handel,

and continues the catalogue for some thirty-five lines more in the

*The poems in Henri Cazalis' volume, *L'Illusion* (Paris, 1888), are an excellent specimen of this use of music. He has many vague musical titles, but the music is always a setting for sentimentality or eroticism. We can identify the music spoken of in only one of his poems—and then only because Saint-Saëns wrote the music—his *Danse Macabre* — after the description in Cazalis' poem.

same vein. English romantic poetry hardly goes beyond a few references to songs. Wordsworth, hearing a Highland girl singing, immediately desires to know "what she sings," i. e., to hear the words of her song.

Throughout the nineteenth century music was a minor art in England, but once or twice it was interestingly treated. De Quincey's *Dream Fugue*[48] was an attempt to use a musical form for literary purposes. An introductory note explains that the essay *The Vision of Sudden Death* and the *Dream-Fugue,* using a theme from it, are to be connected with the previously published paper *The English Mail Coach.* "The ultimate object was the Dream-Fugue, as an attempt to wrestle with the utmost efforts of music in dealing with a colossal form of impassioned horror."

There are other scattered evidences of musical interest before the general awakening towards the end of the century. Felicia Hemans (1793-1835) has a poem[49] on Mozart's *Requiem,* but it is connected with the composer rather than with the music. As early as 1857 an anthology[50] of poems and passages dealing with music was published, and there have been many since that time. Matthew Arnold gives a short description in verse of Beethoven's contrapuntal vocal music (probably the *Kyrie* from the *Missa Solemnis*) in his *Epilogue to Lessing's Laocoön,* a poem discussing the relation of music to poetry.

The position of Browning in England, as poet-musician, may be compared with that of Grillparzer in Germany.[51] It is interesting to notice that Browning's musical references were vague in his early works, and became more specific as his poetic art developed. *A Toccata of Galuppi's* and *Master Hughues of Saxe-Gotha,* both published in 1855, are based on musical topics, but the subject of the first is unidentifiable,[52] and the second, while containing an analysis of a five-part fugue, deals with a fictitious composer. *Abt Vogler* (1864) takes for its subject a genuine composer and treats of his improvisations and his musical philosophy. All three poems use technical terminology freely, but do not refer to specific works. *Fifine at the Fair* (1872) continues the general discussion of music, with technical terms,[53] but becomes specific in its discussion of parts of Schumann's *Carnaval.*[54] The last of the important musical poems, *Parleyings with Charles Avison* (1887), devotes a great deal of attention to a *Grand March* of Avison's. The poem as a whole is a discussion of changes of taste in music, using the *March* as an example. It is analyzed from the point of view of harmony, rhythm, and imagined orchestration. Browning discusses the possibility of modernizing or archaizing it, and suggests the technical means by which these changes could be accomplished. The poem also contains casual references to a number of other musical works.

The influence of Browning doubtless played a large part in producing the flow of musical poems in England towards the close of the century, although the history of the musical lyric in France shows a similar phenomenon, differing only in degree, without any such influence to explain it. At any rate, from about 1870 onwards musical compositions became an increasingly popular subject for poets. Frances Ridley Havergal has a poem[55] on Beethoven's *Moonlight Sonata* containing a lengthy description of the music, and another one entitled *Threefold Praise* treats of Haydn's *Creation*, Mendelssohn's *Elijah*, and Handel's *Messiah*.[56] John Payne published several musical poems between 1870 and 1880. However, at this point single poems cease to deserve mention.

Probably the first person to write a series of poems on pieces of music was the Polish poet, Kornel Ujejski, who, between 1857 and 1860 wrote his *Tlumaczenia Szopena*,[57] a series of eleven poems on works of Chopin. There are two poems on the *Sonata Op. 35* (one on the *Funeral March* and one on the *Finale*), three on different *Preludes*, and six on *Mazurkas*. The opus number of each composition is placed at the beginning of the poem describing it. It is greatly to be doubted whether later English, French, and German writers who published similar series knew Ujejski's work. With the exception of Dehmel, who translated the poem on the *Funeral March* into German, we find no evidence of such knowledge, and collections of musical poetry by a single author did not appear elsewhere until considerably later.

In 1899 Mary Alice Vialls published *Music Fancies and Other Verses*,[58] a collection containing ten sonnets on specific compositions, and one or two other poems with more general subjects, such as *Russian Songs*. Richard Watson Gilder's *A Book of Music*[59] is a similar collection, and the most important book of this type in English is John Todhunter's *Sounds and Sweet Airs*.[60] Since the last two decades of the past century many single poems on musical works have been written.

After 1880 French literature returned to musical subjects.[61] Poems were often called "Nocturnes," "Sonatines," etc., and some of the extremists even attempted a poetry which should replace music. More important is the fact that poems on musical composi-

tions began to be written, although they were never so common
as in England and Germany. In January, 1886, the *Revue wagnérienne* published "Hommage à Wagner," a group of eight sonnets whose authors included Mallarmé Varlaine, René Ghil, and
Edouard Dujardin. Stuart Merrill's *Poèmes (1887-1897)*[62] contains
musical titles and vague references, as well as several verses on
specific works. Henri Allorge's *Le clavier des harmonies*[63] consists
of one hundred and forty-six pages of poetry on music, including
poems on thirty-seven composers, a number of musical forms
(fugue, sonata, quartette, symphony, etc.), and all the instruments
of the orchestra. Surprisingly enough, there is much intelligent
criticism in the section on composers, and a respectable amount
of good poetry scattered throughout the entire book. Various single
poems of importance have appeared since this volume, and there
has been at least one similar collection of verse on composers and
vaguely musical subjects, but without direct references to musical
works.[64]

In modern Germany, also, music has been a favorite subject for
poets. Hans von Wolzogen, who edited the *Bayreuther Blätter,* has
a quantity of poems to Wagner, his family, and his genius, including a series called *Die Sieben Werke.*[65] He also wrote one or two
things on non-Wagnerian music. Ernst Lissauer has cycles of poems
on Beethoven[66] and Bach,[67] and Franz Werfel, Alfred Neumann,
and others have written verses on single works.

The most prolific and most recent of the German musical poets,
however, is Richard Plattensteiner, whose two volumes, *Musica-
lische Gedichte* and *Neue Musikalische Gedichte,* are dedicated to
Beethoven and Schubert respectively, and appeared on the cen-
tenaries of these composers' deaths.[68] Together these volumes contain over twenty-five poems on specific compositions, including a
large number of composers. In addition to these, there are several
poems whose subjects cannot be identified, but which certainly
deal with individual works. Taken all together, this is much the
largest body of verse on music by any one author, but it is not so
interesting as one might wish, since much of it is "interpretation"
of music in terms of stories, scenes, or abstract ideas, and the connection between verse and music is often rather tenuous.

Within the last thirty years a number of authors have written
doggerel on such musical subjects as the lives and works of composers, the plots of operas, and the elements of notation. Most of
these works are unimportant, but at least two deserve mention.

Das Orchester[69] is a semi-serious poem going through the instruments of the orchestra and giving a few verses about each. The anonymous author apparently did not know of Allorge's work, for in the preface he claims originality for the idea of his poem. Vincente Escohotado's *La Musiquea, Poema Cómico*[70] is largely a series of versified biographies of composers, naming most of the works of each.

In this survey of musical literature it has been impossible to include the appearances of music in fiction which have been common since the beginnings of romanticism. Many novels have musical heroes or heroines, and many others use music incidentally. Some authors have used it discriminatingly, but the general rule has been that musical passages are full of the grossest sort of musical heroes or heroines, and many others use music incidentally. errors. Several critics have made amusing collections of these blunders. The lives of composers have frequently been romanticized into novels, Beethoven and Wagner being the chief victims. Some half a dozen works of fiction have been written on the relationship between Wagner and Ludwig II of Bavaria. Most of these works are mere parasitic sentimentality, but the fact that major novelists have made skilful and effective use of music can be illustrated by Romain Rolland's *Jean Christophe,* Tolstoi's *Kreutzer Sonata,* Thomas Mann's *Tristan* and *Dr. Faustus,* d'Annunzio's *Trionfo della morte,* and Franz Werfel's *Verdi* — to name only a few.

The beginnings of the scholarly study of the general relationships between music and literature, and especially of literary treatments of music, should also be mentioned. Though the critics of classical antiquity occasionally touched on these matters, and they were considered at length in some of the eighteenth-century treatises on aesthetics, the systematic study of them really began towards the end of the nineteenth century. Since that time there have been many investigations of the influence of music on individual writers and literary movements, the relationship of text and music in vocal compositions, literary influences on music, the connections between the techniques and aesthetics of the two arts, and their historical parallelism. Some indication of the extent and chronology of this type of study may be seen in the fact that the author's private bibliography of musico-literary relationships now contains approximately 2,200 items, only a handful of which were published before 1880.

CHAPTER II

Imitation of Music in Poetry

In spite of a civilization which has practically ceased to read aloud, poetry consists essentially of sound. It is also an art extending in time rather than in space. Since it shares its sensuous material and its medium of development with music, these two arts are more closely related to each other than either is to painting, sculpture, or architecture, whose material is the visible rather than the audible, and whose existence is in space. Certain analogies between musical and architectural structure have led some writers to state that architecture is the art most closely related to music, but the difference between a simultaneous perception of all the parts and a consecutive development of the structural units seems insuperable. Since the "romantic confusion of the arts," terms of one art have been freely applied to another, and the cultivation of synaesthesia has led to a great multiplication of terms which are recognized in more than one art — a development which has tended towards exaggeration and affectation. Although we shall find several elements which are the common property of poetry and music, the tendency to speak of one in terms of the other has been, in general, confusing.

Cœuroy writes that such words as *melody* and *harmony* become such powerful forces that they may even generate literary movements.[1] Most writers do not define such terms when they use them, and the fact that the "melody" of a verse and its "harmony" are usually synonymous shows that when these words are used with reference to poetry their musical sense is entirely abandoned. Faguet defines the term "harmonious" as he uses it:

J'appele harmonieuse une phrase qui, par les sonorités ou les assourdissements
des mots, par la langueur ou la vigeur des rythmes, par toutes sortes d'artifices,
naturels, du reste, dans la disposition des mots et des membres de phrases,
représente un sentiment, peint la pensée par les sons, et la mêle ainsi plus
profondément à notre sensibilité.[2]

I call a passage harmonious if, by the sonority or muffling effects of words,
by the languor or vigor of rhythms, by all sorts of natural devices in the ar-
rangement of words and phrases, it represents a sentiment, paints the thought
by means of the sound, and thus impresses the idea more deeply on our
sensibility.

It is evident that his use of the word has nothing to do with its
musical sense, but he is more exact than the average writer, who
seems to use both "melody" and "harmony" as synonyms for "eu-
phony." Similarly, verse is often described as "musical," but we
cannot imagine anyone who would enjoy a reading in a language
which he could not understand (this would ensure its being heard
as pure sound, stripped of the meaning arbitrarily attached to
words) with the same degree, or even the same type of enjoyment
as a musician derives from a symphony.

In spite of these verbal confusions, there are certain musical
elements in the structure of poetry which enable it, to a limited
extent, to imitate and reproduce the effects of music.

Poetry contains a great deal of imitation of all kinds. The fact
that actions may be suggested and ideas represented by imitative
effects in verse is shown by Faguet's analysis of a fable of La Fontaine in terms of his imitative "harmony." The simplest type of
musical imitation is achieved by the invention of words which
will sound as much as possible like the sound which the poet wishes
to suggest. If these words are really needed, they will become a
regular part of the language; if not, they will remain imitative
sounds which cannot properly be called words at all. In either case,
onomatopoetic words are essentially not a description of sound, but
an imitation of it, and we find them used in this capacity in various
poems on music.

Description by imitative words is, however, sadly inadequate,
for it admits of no sounds not existing in whatever language the
poet happens to be using. A comparison of "kikeriki," "cocorico"
or "coquerico," "cuccuruccù," and "cock-a-doodle-doo" shows almost perfect agreement as to the consonant, but a wide difference
in vowels, though it may be remarked that any consonant which
may exist in a cock's crow is negligible. A person familiar with all

four of these versions of it might easily fail to recognize the imitation given by the oboe in Saint-Saëns' *Danse Macabre*.

The sounds of both musical instruments and vowels are differentiated largely by their timbre, but the vowels have timbres of their own which do not correspond to those of any instruments. Most consonants are noises rather than tones. These facts sufficiently explain why imitation of music by words invented for the purpose is necessarily inadequate and usually comical. Also, we can now see why percussion instruments — drums, triangles, cymbals, etc. — are the most frequently imitated. They, like the consonants, produce noise, and hence they can easily be suggested by the proper consonants. Liliencron is particularly fond of the effects of percussion instruments, which he always imitates with a comic effect. *Die Musik Kommt*[3] is a good example. It is a clever poem describing the march of a regimental band through a sleepy village. It opens:

> Klingling, bumbum und tschingdada,
> Zieht im Triumph der Perserschah?
> Und um die Ecke brausend bricht's
> Wie Tubaton des Weltgerichts.

> Kling-ling, boom-boom, and ching-da-da——
> A triumph of the Persian Shah?
> It rounds the corner with a boom
> Like trumpets of the Day of Doom.

Throughout the entire poem the music is kept before us by the occasional use of such imitative words, and the effect of the crescendo of the band's approach and the diminuendo of its retreat is reproduced, until the poem closes with the final restoration of the *status quo*.

Many authors have imitated various instruments and some of their imitations have become literary commonplaces. The sound of the trumpet has a lineage of twenty centuries from Ennius' "At tuba terribili sonitu *taratantara* dixit"[4] to the policemen's chorus in *The Pirates of Penzance*. Both Goethe and Henri Cazalis have imitated, in widely different sounds, the violin, and a list of the poets who have attempted this could be extended almost indefinitely. We may say, however, that, if we except the percussion instruments, it is almost impossible to find a verbal imitation of any instrument so accurate that we could recognize it if we were not told what it is supposed to represent.

More subtle and more effective is the use of words which are selected and arranged with a view to suggesting a musical effect by the sound of an entire passage. Vowel sounds are largely used for this purpose, though the avoidance of certain consonants is helpful in a negative way. Paul Verlaine's *Chanson d'automne*[5] certainly gives something of the effect of a violin playing slowly in its lower register:

> Les sanglots longs
> Des violoons
>   De l'automne
> Blessent mon cœur
> D'une langueur
>   Monotone.

A similar attempt at transcribing music for poetry was made by Théodore de Banville in his poem on *La dernière pensée de Weber* (1845).

Le poème qui porte ce nom s'essaie, par la variété des rythmes, à rendre le caractère de la musique, notamment grâce à un refrain quatre fois répété. Il ne cherche pas seulement à exprimer le sentiment de la phrase musicale: il veut que par le rythme poétique soit recréée l'impression sonore.[6]

This poem attempts by the variety of its rhythms to reproduce the character of the music, especially by the use of a refrain which is repeated four times. It not only seeks to express the sentiment of the musical work: it tries to make the poetic rhythm recreate the sound.

This refrain,

> Nuit d'étoiles,
> Sous tes voiles,
> Sous ta brise et tes parfums,
> Triste lyre
> Qui suspire,
> Je rêve aux amours défunts,

does not succeed so well as the stanza of Verlaine quoted above, and Cœuroy's claim that it reproduces to some extent the particular quality of the waltz in question seems unjustified. These imitations of musical sound in words are at best vague, and require definite verbal ideas to guide them. If violins were not mentioned one could easily take Verlaine's verse as a representation of horns, and as a matter of fact it may be mentioned that horns are imitated, in his *Nuit de Walpurgis classique,* by a similar selection and gradation of sounds. De Vigny's famous opening line of *Le Cor,*

"J'aime le son du Cor, le soir, au fond des bois," seems to suggest the horn timbre inevitably, but if all suggestion of verbal meanings is ignored, it will do as well for violins, just as Verlaine's lines might be equally effective for a horn. Similarly, if the title of Banville's poem were suppressed we could not even know that it applies to a waltz at all, much less to any particular one.

The attempt to imitate the sounds of music in poetry is not, then, successful in so far as the reproduction of any specific piece of music is concerned, or even the unmistakable suggestion of any particular instrument. But it can be highly effective if we are told what is being represented and if the imitative passage is not too long. Under these conditions the sound of the verse helps to develop and hold an idea which the words have already stated.

The call of the cuckoo offers a particularly interesting case of verbal imitation of music. The cuckoo's is one of the very few bird-calls which can be represented accurately on our musical scale, and probably the only one which is simple enough to be generally recognized and exactly imitated. Thus whenever anyone, in describing a piece of music, speaks of the call of the cuckoo, or whenever a "hearer" interprets a composition as a scene involving a cuckoo, we expect a conspicuous use of the descending major third. It is convenient here to consider this use of the cuckoo as actual imitation of the music, for anyone reading at all expressively would naturally make something of an imitation of the bird where his call occurred. In a poem on Beethoven's *Sixth Symphony*[7] Plattensteiner uses this call to get in one of the standard and stale allusions to cuckoldry, and John Payne confuses us with it in a poem on Field's *Nocturne in D Minor* when he says:

> Our hearts have all forgot the spell
> That held the summer noon;
> We echo back the cuckoo's knell,
> And not the linnet's tune.[8]

We look in vain for the cuckoo's call in the *Nocturne;* he has simply stumbled upon it as a symbol of melancholy in autumn, in contrast to the linnet's song, which he had used as a symbol of summer in a previous poem[9] on Wagner's *Tristan und Isolde.*

A very exact piece of musical imitation is found in Ujejski's use of the cuckoo in combination with exact rhythmical imitation of the music. He interprets Chopin's *Mazurka, Op. 30, No. 2* as a little girl resenting her aunt's determination to chaperone her and keep her in order. The girl goes to the garden to consult a popular

oracle in the form of the cuckoo, which is supposed to call once for
every year before her marriage. Then we have her question and
her meditations, alternating with the answer of the bird:

> Gadajże mi — *kuku!*
> Króciusieńko, — *kuku!*
> Już mam dosyć — *kuku!*
> Kukuleńko! — *kuku!*
> To ptaszysko — *kuku!*
> W uszach wierci, — *kuku!*
> Krzycz-że sobie — *kuku!*
> Aż do śmierci! — *kuku!*

> Tell me — *cuckoo!*
> Very shortly — *cuckoo!*
> That's enough — *cuckoo!*
> My little birdie, — *cuckoo!*
> This bad bird — *cuckoo!*
> Irritates my ears — *cuckoo!*
> Cry yourself — *cuckoo!*
> Until death! — *cuckoo!*

This finds its exact counterpart in the music, and anyone not
familiar with the *Mazurka* could form an accurate idea of the middle section from this interpretation of it. The left hand fills in with
chords in a regular waltz pattern, and the melody is as follows:

The last note leads back into the first section, and the poem changes
back to its original rhythm and continues to follow the form of
the music.

Poetry can imitate musical rhythms much better than it can
suggest timbre or pitch, but the possibilities of rhythmical imitation have been strangely neglected. Rhythm is the one element
which often exists in identical forms in both music and poetry,
and most of the effects of musical rhythm are possible, in a more

limited way, in poetry. Duple and triple time, syncopation, and
even rests are a regular part of the technique of verse; hence we
should expect poets who try to imitate music to take full advantage of them. If the general rhythmic pattern of a composition is
followed, and if its more conspicuous changes of rhythm are reproduced in verse, the transcription of the music effect will be
much aided. The comparatively rare poems which use this method
demonstrate its effectiveness conclusively, but neglect of the similarities of musical and poetic rhythm has been the general rule.
The Viennese waltz relies on its rhythm for most of its effect, yet
authors often describe it in inappropriate meters and therefore fail
to give the impression of the music at all. Catherine Parmenter
deals with *The Blue Danube* in a sonnet,[11] and Richard Plattensteiner interprets Josef Strauss' *Mein Lebenslauf ist Lieb und
Lust*[12] in three stanzas of strongly accented iambic pentameter, beginning:

> Die Erde war für mich ein Paradies,
> Da sie die Liebe birgt vieledler Frauen,
> Ich möchte gern in ihre Augen schauen,
> Das war es, das mich immer singen hiess.

Sacheverell Sitwell's *Valse Estudiantina* is in free verse with a predominantly iambic pattern.[13]

Sometimes, however, poets have followed the rhythm of the
waltz. Plattensteiner has another poem called *Letzter Walzer*,[14]
and a line or two will show how much better than his other attempt this one captures the spirit of a Viennese waltz:

> Sie blieben noch immer umschlungen,
> Wär leise der Walzer verklungen . . . .

There are other examples of triple meters used to describe waltzes,
but, strangely enough, poets treating the waltz in general seem to
take more care to match meter and subject than do those who set
out to describe some particular example of the form.

One of the most interesting experiments in this direction is
Amy Lowell's *After Hearing a Waltz by Bartók*.[15] This poem gives
the meditations — or perhaps the ravings would be more accurate — of a man who has just murdered a rival at a dance. The
crime was committed in an upstairs room while a waltz was being
played below, and the waltz-music and the killing have become
inextricably entangled in the murderer's mind. The entire poem
is in dactylic and anapestic meters, and these are so strongly

marked that it would be an easy task to write out the time of the
entire poem in musical notation, in spite of irregularities indi-
cating rests and syncopation. The first two lines may be noted:

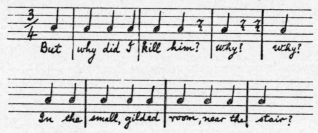

In the fifth stanza the time is counted out, "One! Two! Three!",
and throughout the remainder of the poem it comes in with increasing frequency, until it dominates the whole. It must be admitted that the meter tends to fall into an anapestic scheme,
making it difficult to read the counting of time, which usually
comes at the beginning of a line, without placing the accent on
"Three!" Once, in next to the last stanza, syncopation is clearly
indicated. The last two stanzas may be quoted to show this syncopation and to illustrate the persistency of the waltz-idea at the
end of the poem.

> And his blood has dripped into my heart!
>   And my heart beats and labours. One! Two!
> Three! His dead limbs have coiled every part
>   Of my body in tentacles. Through
>   My ears the waltz jangles. Like glue
> His dead body holds me athwart.
>
> One! Two! Three! Give me air! Oh! My God!
>   One! Two! Three! I am drowning in slime!
> One! Two! Three! And his corpse, like a clod,
>   Beats me into a jelly. The chime
>   One! Two! Three! And his dead limbs keep time.
> Air! Give me air! Air! My God!

In order to appreciate the full effect of this persistent, reiterated
beat, this tripping rhythm combined with a gruesome idea, one
should read the entire poem, for its eleven stanzas have a highly
cumulative effect.

The Elizabethan lyrics written for definite tunes followed the
rhythms of the various dance forms far more closely than poems
have done since the seventeenth century. Waller has a poem

"Made to a Saraband," and Ben Jonson, in *The Staple of News,*
shows us a poetaster who wrote verses for popular tunes.[16] This
amusement has continued to the present day,[17] but poets merely
writing about music have seldom followed its meter. Often the
names of dance forms are used for no apparent reason in the titles
of poems. Edith Sitwell has a number of these titles, and they seem
to have no more connection with the musical rhythms than could
be explained on the basis of pure chance. Her *Polka* and a *Fox
Trot*[18] have no discoverable relation to these dance forms. A
Waltz[19] is, for the most part, dactylic and anapestic, and a
Mazurka[20] is largely iambic, although a few lines are properly
dactylic, agreeing with the ¾ or ⅜ time of the mazurka. The last
line ends, as a mazurka should end, on the second beat of the bar:
"The Fourth, such flames we know not here, dear!" Many other
writers have made a similar use of musical titles, usually with bad
effect. A person who understands the musical forms in question is
naturally irritated by misleading titles, and one who does not
understand them can expect to receive nothing beyond the creation of a vague musical "atmosphere."

Ujejski's poems on Chopin show a more careful use of rhythm
than any others. Each of them is based on a definite composition,
and may be recited or sung to it. Changes in rhythm are followed
by changes in meter, and the ABA form of many of the pieces is
indicated by a different poetic form in the middle section. The
basic rhythm is also faithfully imitated, as is necessary in a poem
which can be sung to the music, and thus we find the mazurka
rhythm in several poems. In *Terkota,*[21] for example, several of
the stanzas end with the quick 1, **2,** 3, followed by 1, **2,** which is
characteristic of the mazurka: "O Jezu najslodszy! — jest ptak!"

It is even possible that Edith Sitwell may have had in her mind
and imitated specific examples of the dance forms which she mentions, although the rhythms of dance forms are so fixed that this
is extremely doubtful. However, rhythms can be imitated by
meters which do not, at a glance, seem to apply. Frances Ridley
Havergal gives very well the impression of the second movement
of Beethoven's *Moonlight Sonata,* which is in ¾ time, by the use
of iambic meter. She begins the movement:

> Awake! Awake!
>> For life is sweet:
> Awake! Awake!
>> New hopes to greet.[22]

Since the use of sustained notes and rests gives the opening of this movement a decidedly iambic character, these lines are well suited to the first bars:

The only possible criticism is that the repeated "Awake!" might be better in the second and fourth lines, where it would coincide with the staccato phrases. The poem goes on in a similar meter, introducing some variations:

> The shadows are fleeting,
>   The substance is sure;
> The joys thou art meeting
>   Shall ever endure.
> Awake! Awake!
>   For twilight now
> That veiled the lake
>   Where dark woods bow,
> In moonlight resplendent
>   Is passing away;
> For brightness ascendant
>   Turns night into day.

Here we have a phenomenon which we shall meet again and again in almost all attempts at poetical treatment of any of the larger musical forms. The opening bars of a movement can readily be described, interpreted, or imitated almost note by note, but the complications of musical form soon outrun the possibilities of poetic treatment, and before long we find the poet lost, so far as the music is concerned, and going off on his own tack, keeping the composition in mind only vaguely, if at all. In the example just quoted the general rhythmic effect is kept, but the complications of the music, with some voices holding while others change or have rests, makes exact poetic imitation impossible.

In Todhunter's *In A Gondola*[23] we have an example of imitation both of rhythm and, suggestively, of a diminuendo effect, and these are both combined with an interpretation suggested by the title. The poem deals with a *Gondola Song* of Mendelssohn, and is definite enough in its imitation and suggestions to identify the work as *Op. 19, No. 6.* The closing lines of the poem,

> And the pulse of the car, swept through silvery spray,
> Dies away in the gloom, dies away — dies away —
> Dies away — dies away!

are clearly a direct imitation of the concluding bars:

In the larger musical forms poets frequently make no attempt at any imitative use of rhythm, even to suggest the predominant rhythmic scheme in cases where it is strongly marked and could easily be followed. Thus Plattensteiner, in his poem on Beethoven's *Seventh Symphony,*[24] uses the same trochaic tetrameter, with occasional irregularities, for both the second and the third movements. The second is an *Allegretto* dominated throughout by a single rhythmic figure of two bars: ♩ ♫ | ♩ ♩ or, in the middle section, ♩ ♫ | ♩ ♫. The third movement, *Presto,* is a *Minuet* which is really a *Scherzo* and has a trio considerably slower than the first theme. (The metronome marks indicate a change from ♩. = 132 to ♩. = 84.) Also, this impression of slower movement is increased by the fact that the trio consists largely of sustained notes, while the minuet has running quarter-notes. The unsuitability of an almost unvarying "Hiawatha meter" for the description of these three widely different rhythmical units is obvious. However, this case is by no means exceptional.

Strictly speaking, counterpoint is impossible in any literary work which is to be read, for two texts cannot be read at the same time. Nevertheless, one finds a few attempts at it. One of the most elaborate may serve as an example both of the nature of these efforts and of their inevitable failure. In a novel entitled *La nuit kurde,* Jean Richard Bloch comments on the impossibility of presenting, in a single line of narrative, the activities of the mind, which works independently on several levels at once. Later, when he comes to a dialogue, he repeats his complaint, taking the mind of a person at a concert (the musical connection is important) as an example. He then goes on to present his dialogue in six columns, printed parallel — one column each for the dreams, the thoughts, and the words of each of the two speakers.[25] Theoretically, of course, this is fine, but in practice the reader cannot take in these six columns simultaneously, and simply has to read them alternately. More often, we find simultaneous speeches on the stage, where they can be spoken by different persons and heard at the same time. Here the mechanics of the thing are workable and something like musical counterpoint might possibly be achieved, but in practice such speeches are ludicrous and are employed largely for comic effects.*

Conrad Aiken has advanced an elaborate theory of poetical counterpoint, and has attempted to put it into practice:

What I had been at the outset somewhat doubtfully hankering for was some way of getting contrapuntal effects in poetry — the effects of contrasting and conflicting tones and themes, a kind of underlying simultaneity in dissimilarity. It seemed to me that by using a large medium, dividing it into several parts, and subdividing these parts into short movements in various veins and forms, this was rendered possible. I do not wish to press the musical analogies too closely. I am aware that the word symphony, as a musical term, has a very definite meaning, and I am aware that it is only with considerable license that I use the term for such poems as *Senlin* or *Forslin,* which have three and five parts respectively, and do not in any orthodox way develop their themes. But the effect obtained is, very roughly speaking, that of the symphony or symphonic poem. Granted that one has chosen a theme — or been chosen by a theme! — which will permit rapid changes of tone, which

---

*Polyphonic vocal music, of course, often has its texts different or overlapping, and polytextuality was once far more extensive than it has been in any music now regularly performed. At one period of its history the motet regularly had independent texts for the different voices, and these texts were frequently in different languages. A strange utilitarian application of polytextuality is found in some of the late mediaeval English masses. As the music became more elaborate, the mass began to take up too much time. But by dividing the text of such longer portions as the Credo and the Gloria between two voices singing simultaneously, the composer made it possible to whip through them in half the time. — See Gustave Reese, *Music in the Middle Ages* (New York, 1940), p. 421.

will not insist on a tone too static, it will be seen that there is no limit to the variety of effects obtainable: for not only can one use all the simpler poetic tones . . . ; but, since one is using them as parts of a larger design, one can also obtain novel effects by placing them in juxtaposition as consecutive movements. . . .

All this, I must emphasize, is no less a matter of emotional tone than of form; the two things cannot well be separated. For such symphonic effects one employs what one might term emotion-mass with just as deliberate a regard for its position in the total design as one would employ a variation of form. One should regard this or that emotional theme as a musical unit having such-and-such a tone-quality, and use it only when that particular tone-quality is wanted. Here I flatly give myself away as being in reality in quest of a sort of absolute poetry, a poetry in which the intention is not so much to arouse an emotion merely, or to persuade of a reality, as to employ such emotion or sense of reality (tangentially struck) with the same cool detachment with which a composer employs notes or chords. Not content to present emotions or things or sensations for their own sakes — as is the case with most poetry — this method takes only the most delicately evocative aspects of them, makes them a keyboard, and plays upon them a music of which the chief characteristic is its elusiveness, its fleetingness, and its richness in shimmering overtones of hint and suggestion. Such a poetry, in other words, will not so much present an idea as use its resonance.[26]

This statement has been given at some length because it is important for the poetic imitation of counterpoint, theme and variations, sonata form, and musical effects in general. It is more or less a summary of the things attempted by those poets who turn to music for their technical inspiration. As far as a strict literary equivalent of counterpoint is concerned, however, we need consider it only briefly. In his reminder that the musical analogy must not be pressed too far, Aiken is aware that he has nowhere suggested any means of securing a true simultaneity of parts. The methods which he suggests may be considered as analogous to the development and variation of a theme, to Beethoven's characteristic sudden changes from *piano* to *fortissimo,* or to the common passages in which a motif is tossed back and forth between the strings and the wood-winds, but they can never correspond to counterpoint in the musical sense of the term.

The drama would seem to be a more legitimate field than lyric poetry for experiments of this type, and Otto Ludwig has formulated a theory of contrapuntal drama and experimented with it.[27] The existence of a principal plot and at least one under-plot gives the necessary material for contrapuntal development, and the drama has the great advantage of being able to present more than one thing at a time. Two or more plots can be under way on the stage at the same moment, and clever technique can keep before an audience the fact that other characters are busy elsewhere while scenes are progressing on the stage. Similarly, dialogue can show each character following his own bent while fitting in with the general conversation. Ludwig developed the idea of contrapuntal dialogue comparatively late, and it is interesting to note that O'Neill's *Strange Interlude* makes use of a similar device. Ludwig was a musician as well as a writer, and he wavered between the two arts. His musical training made him follow musical forms with an accuracy unheard of in most writers who attempt to use musical technique. *Der Erbförster* (1853) is his most outstanding attempt at the adaptation of the principles of polyphonic music to the stage. Characters, like musical themes, present themselves under different aspects, showing variations and modulations in a musical way, and Ludwig insisted that they should conform to all the laws of music. In the fifth act

L'opposition entre le mode majeur du début et le mode mineur du dénouement est même si crue, et si peu conforme au système classique de développement symphonique, que Ludwig, très attaché aux formes orthodoxes, se l'est reprochée plus tard comme une faute de composition.[28]

The contrast between the major mode of the opening and the minor mode of the conclusion is even so blunt and so out of keeping with the classic system of symphonic development that Ludwig, with his great devotion to orthodox forms, later condemned it as an error of composition.

However, it would seem that any drama must necessarily be, to a certain extent, "contrapuntal," and Ludwig's theories probably injured his literary art.

Il n'est pas douteux que la hantise des formes musicales n'ait nui parfois au dramaturge au lieu de le secourir. Etablir un contrepoint, régler la marche des parties, les compliquer, les enlacer, c'est une des jouissances intellectuelles les plus aiguës qui se puissent concevoir. Mais à transposer cette méthode au drame on risque la complication et l'obscurité. C'est l'écueil qui n'a pas évité Ludwig. Ses pièces sont extraordinairement encombrées de quiproquos, d'événements qui s'enchevêtrent au point d'en rendre le récit presque impossible. Le contrepoint en est la cause, et sans doute est-ce la vengeance de la Musique sur celui que, pendant près de trente années, elle crut s'être attaché à jamais.[29]

It is obvious that the preoccupation with musical forms sometimes injured the dramatist instead of helping him. To establish a counterpoint, control the leading of the different voices, complicate them, interweave them, is one of the keenest imaginable intellectual pleasures. But in transferring this method to the drama there is a danger of complication and obscurity. Ludwig could not steer clear of this reef. His plays are extraordinarily encumbered with confusions, with events which are so entangled that it is practically impossible to summarize them. Counterpoint is responsible, and this is doubtless the vengeance of Music on a man whom, for nearly thirty years, she had thought to be hers forever.

Poetry is most successful in imitating musical effects when it confines itself to those elements which exist in succession and gives up the attempt to reproduce anything resembling harmony or counterpoint. Music constantly repeats phrases with changes at each appearance, and this procedure extends from the simplest musical periods, built on a repetition of phrases, to the most complicated examples of fugue and sonata form. It is especially conspicuous in the compositions or movements using a theme and variations. This technique of variation can be easily enough applied in poetry, and it is one of the standard devices of such forms as the ballad, with its varied repetition, and the many types of lyrics with refrains. It is also used, to a lesser extent, in the larger poetical forms. The reiteration of "Thrones, Dominations, Virtues, Princedoms, Powers" in *Paradise Lost* has something of the effect of a musical motif, and an even better example is to be found in Swinburne's *Tristram of Lyonesse*.[30] Swinburne is describing Iseult's vigil and her thoughts of Tristram as she sits in a castle by the sea. The theme of the storm on the ocean is given out at considerable length at its first appearance:

> And the night spake, and thundered on the sea,
> Ravening aloud for ruin of lives: and all
> The bastions of the main cliff's northward wall
> Rang response out from all their deepening length,
> As the east wind girded up his godlike strength
> And hurled in hard against that high-towered hold
> The fleeces of the flock that knows no fold,
> The rent white shreds of shattering storm: but she
> Heard not nor heeded wind or storming sea,
> Knew not if night were mild or mad with wind.

After this introduction the storm is kept before us by a two-line motif of wind and sea recurring again and again in the midst of her soliloquy, and each time taking her recent thoughts as the theme of its similes. Thus we have

> And swordlike was the sound of iron wind,
> And as a breaking battle was the sea,

and

> And all her soul was as the breaking sea,
> And all her heart anhungered as the wind,

and, again,

> And as man's anguish clamouring cried the wind,
> And as God's anger answering rang the sea.

The seven appearances of this couplet, each one varied to suit its context, are amazingly effective, and the passage is an excellent illustration of how the musical method of varying a theme can be applied as a legitimate poetic device. As Swinburne was essentially unmusical, it is extremely unlikely that he was consciously using a method borrowed from music, although the extent of the theme and variations here is certainly far beyond that commonly found in poetry.

Swinburne used a varied theme for a particular passage in a larger work, but several writers have attempted the theme and variations, admittedly borrowed from music, as an independent form of verse.[31] The chief difficulty lies in giving each variation its own distinctive character, as in music, and thus preventing the set from becoming merely repetitious. In recent years two different solutions of the problem have been attempted, with reasonably successful results. Josef Weinheber wrote several sets of the ordinary literary type of repetitious variations,[32] but his *Variationen auf eine hölderlinische Ode*[33] is entirely different. It begins by simply quoting its theme — Hölderlin's famous short ode *An die Parzen*. The first variations are entirely formal, each reworking the poem into a different metrical or stanzaic form with as little alteration of the original wording as possible. Then come several variations of content, each viewing the idea of the ode from a different and clearly defined point of view. Then follow three developments of single phrases into independent poems of different forms. After these the farthest point of departure is reached in a striking piece of virtuosity, an entirely new poem made by a complete rearrangement of all the words — no less and no more — of Hölderlin's poem. This immediately precedes the final variation, another metrical one which returns close to the original theme. I have encountered no other literary variations which produce the effect of the musical form as do these of Weinheber.

A different solution has been attempted by E. H. W. Meyerstein.[34] His theme — an original one — is a sort of skeleton of a fairy-tale about a king who lived in a house of glass. Each of the variations is then a different allegorical interpretation, from a different point of view and in a different form, of the simple facts of the story as presented in the theme.

Since a theme may be so easily varied in poetry, it is natural that this technique should be borrowed by writers to imitate similar developments in the music they attempt to describe, and we have examples ranging all the way from the mere echoing of a phrase to the elaborate literary imitation of a fantasy in the form of a theme and variations, and even of a five-part fugue.

The reiteration of a phrase, in a manner suggesting musical treatment, is fairly common in poems with musical subjects. There can be no doubt that this is the purpose of such lines as

> Where thy soul not afraid,
> Though all alone unlonely,
> Wanders and wavers, wavers wandering.[35]

The same method is used in d'Annunzio's sonnet *Ancora Sopra l' "Erotik"* (of Grieg):[36]

> Erinni! È questo il tragico tuo nome.
> Ancora è viva in te l'antica possa.
> L'immenso notte, o Furia, s'è commossa
> tutta al fremito sol de le tue chiome.
> Se appari tu su la mia soglia come
> una fiamma fiammendo ne la rossa
> veste, mi corre un brivido per l'ossa,
> l'anima grida il tragico tuo nome.

Erinnys! This is your tragic name. The ancient power still lives in you. Immense night, O Fury, is troubled at the mere rustle of your tresses. If you appear on my threshold like a flame flaming in a red garment, a shudder runs through my bones; my soul screams out your tragic name.

The "fiamma fiammendo" suggests a phrase with its echo, and the repetition of "il tragico tuo nome" suggests the form of the music and tells us that the poet has come in his interpretation to the point where the first half of the piece is repeated, an octave lower, with imitative echoing of the phrases in a lower voice. In accordance with the musical structure, the sestet presents the idea in a different light.

Frances Ridley Havergal was attempting to describe and imitate simultaneously when, in describing the *Adagio* of the *Moonlight Sonata,* she wrote some of the world's worst lines:[37]

> Loving and longing, loving and yearning,
> With a hidden flow of electric burning
> Ever returning;
> Meeting again in a calm repeat,
> Slow and sweet,
> Sweet and slow.

Poetical imitation of musical variation is applied to whole sections as well as to individual phrases. D'Annunzio's poem *Sopra un "Adagio" di Johannes Brahms*[38] is a good example. The first stanza is as follows:

> Tutto è silenzio, lùgubre infinito
> Silenzio, nel lontano
> regno che regenerai. Simile a un nero
> sepolcro è un trono vacuo, deserto
> de tempo immemorabile, fatale:
> ove già stette solitario assiso
> un re omnipotente.

All is silence, sad, infinite silence, in the distant realm which you shall rule. Like a black sepulchre stands an empty throne, vacant for immemorial years, fatal — a throne where formerly an omnipotent king sat alone.

The next two stanzas develop the theme of this king's past glory, and then there is a return to a slightly changed repetition of the opening, followed by a two-line coda:

> E scomparve. Sta un lugubre infinito
> silenzio sul lontano
> regno che regnerai; ed un mistero
> profondo, come in un sepolcro operto,
> troverai tu nel trono, o spiritale
> regina di quel morto paradiso
> che tace eternamente,
>
> o vana luce di quel paradiso
> morte ne la mia mente!

It has vanished. There is a sad, infinite silence over the distant realm which you shall rule; and you will find a profound mystery, as in an open sepulchre, in the throne, O spirit-queen of this dead, eternally silent paradise — O vain light of this paradise dead in my mind!

The *Adagio* is not identified, but there can be no doubt as to the general lines of its structure.

Plattensteiner supplies another good example. In a Beethoven poem entitled *Quartett Opus Nr. 135*[39] he interprets the first movement:

Grüne Fluren hingegossen
Baden sich im Sonnenschein,
Lächelnd wogen hin und her
Hohe Halme, in den Himmel tauchend. —
Sorglos heiter lasst uns freuen,
Auf der schönen, bunten Erde
Wie im Spiegel uns erkennend:
Lächelnd wogend hin und her,
Hohen Halmen gleich, die tauchen
Stark und froh in ihren Himmel. —

Green, flowing meadows bask in the sunshine. Smiling fields of tall grain
wave to and fro, shooting up towards the sky. — Let us rejoice, carefree and
cheerful, on the lovely, gay earth, recognizing ourselves as in a mirror: smil-
ingly waving to and fro, like high stalks of grain which shoot up, strong and
happy, towards the sky.

These imitations of variations on a theme are merely incidental,
but the theme and variations has been used at length, both as an
independent literary form and as an imitation of the musical
form. Browning's *The Ring and the Book,* which tells the same
story several times, each repetition being a different character's
version of it, is simply a set of variations on a theme, and it is
probable that Browning, with his musical and poetic gifts, deliberately set out to combine the two arts in this form. A comparison of the work to an Andante, a few lines before the end of the
poem, supports this view.

An extended and extremely clever imitation of a musical theme
and variations is to be found in George Sand's *Le Contrebandier.*[40]
It is introduced by a few pages telling how a friend of hers once
heard Liszt play his *Rondo fantastique* on the Spanish song *El contrabandista,* and afterwards remarked that it made him see an
entire drama. The company laughed at him and asked him to reproduce it.

Il se récusa d'abord, parce que la musique instrumentale ne peut jamais avoir
un sens arbitraire; mais le compositeur lui ayant permis de s'abandonner à
son imagination, il prit la plume en riant et traduisit son rêve dans une
forme qu'il appela lyrico-fantastique, faute d'un autre nom, et qui après tout
n'est pas plus neuve que tout ce qu'on invente aujourd'hui.

He declined at first, because instrumental music can never have an arbitrary
meaning; but when the composer had given him permission to surrender to
his imagination, he laughingly took his pen and translated his dream into
a form which, for lack of a better name, he called lyrico-fantastic, and which,
after all, is no newer than most of the things that are invented nowadays.

His interpretation follows. A company sit in a garden feasting and
singing the song *Yo que soy contrabandista*. A stranger arrives and
claims to be a rightful member of the party. Being challenged to
sing the song as a proof that he is a native of the district, he makes
several attempts, always substituting some other word for *contrebandier*. Each time he is rebuked and told to sing it correctly if
he wishes to establish his identity. He goes on and on, substituting
in turn *chevrier, écolier, amant infortuné, meurtrier, guerrier,
aventurier, eremite,* and *poète couronné.* Each time he alters the
words and the mood of the song to suit the condition in which
he has placed himself, and after each version there is a general
outbreak of reproof, mixed with a convivial refrain from the entire company. Finally, the stranger makes a prayer in which he
connects all the men he has claimed to be into a logical sequence.
He then departs, singing the song correctly, and as he disappears
in the distance the banqueters suddenly recognize him as the
leader of the smugglers — the hero of the song — whom it is their
duty to arrest. The entire piece, with its varied returns of one
theme and the boisterous interludes between them, is a brilliant
piece of work and succeeds remarkably well in giving the reader
the effect of Liszt's *Rondo.*

Imitation of the recurring theme has gone beyond the theme-
and-variations form, however, in the most striking literary adaptation of the fugue, De Quincey's *Dream Fugue.*[41] This work not
only shows remarkable ingenuity in discovering literary equivalents for the structural devices of contrapuntal music; it also
achieves the cumulative excitement and final synthesis of a great
fugue. This success is due not merely to the general structure,
but to the stylistic details as well, for the entire work is written
in an ornate poetic prose relying heavily on balance and antithesis,
varied repetition, and other devices which music and literature
have in common. Though De Quincey demonstrated conclusively
that, at least under special circumstances, the fugue could be effectively adapted for literary purposes, few other writers have
attempted it. The literary fugue in Joyce's *Ulysses* is almost purely
an intellectual exercise and a *tour de force,* and Delmore
Schwartz's *The Repetitive Heart: Eleven Poems in Imitation of
the Fugue Form* [43] contains nothing in imitation of the fugue
form.

If attempts at fugue and other polyphonic forms have been
rare, the poets have made up for this neglect by their experiments

with sonata-form. Perhaps they have realized that the impossibility of reading more than one thing at a time makes poetry incapable of really reproducing any contrapuntal or polyphonic forms of music. This difficulty still holds, of course, in the combination of themes found in sonata-form, but here it is at least of secondary importance. The essential element of sonata-form, the statement and development of two main contrasting themes, can be effected in poetry also. In a small form, it is the principle upon which the sonnet is constructed, and it must be admitted that most writers of verbal sonatas and symphonies do not go far beyond what the sonnet accomplished. They state the contrasting themes and give something of their relationship to each other, but usually either skip the development section or become hopelessly entangled in it. Thematic development, like imitative rhythm, is too limited in poetry to follow accurately its musical uses.

We may immediately discard a number of poems which bear the name "symphony," but make no attempt to use the musical form. Perhaps the most famous of these is Gautier's *Symphonie en blanc majeur,* which has only one theme, is concerned entirely with visual imagery, and uses one fixed verse-form throughout. Aiken's statement that he was in search of a symphonic poetry should also not be taken too literally: he wished to create various musical effects, most of which are to be found in symphonies, but he had no intention of writing in strict — or even loose — symphonic form.

Among those who have really attempted to use symphonic form in poetry are John Gould Fletcher, Henry Van Dyke, A. E. G. Legge, Grace Hazard Conkling, Madeleine Merens-Melmer, John Todhunter, and Richard Plattensteiner. Some of these experimenters have even gone so far as to give Italian directions for tempo and to indicate the tonality of the various movements. References to music are frequently employed to keep the reader's mind occupied with the musical analogy. Indications of tonalities for the movements are sometimes given,[43] but we more often find the tempo specified, as in Arthur Legge's *A Symphony,*[44] with its *Andante, Adagio, Scherzo,* and *Allegro.* The Italian directions in John Gould Fletcher's *Sand and Spray; A Sea-Symphony*[45] change with every new subject (and there are six in the second movement alone), and apply to the subjects themselves more than to anything in the poet's treatment of them. Thus the second movement is:

1.	Sailboats	Scherzando.
2.	The Tide	Con moto ondeggiante.
3.	The Sands	Lento, appassionata.
4.	The Gulls	Molto allegro.
5.	Steamers	Maestoso.
6.	Night of Stars	Allegro brilliante.

Fletcher has also written a number of verse "symphonies" on different colors.

For the purposes of this study, these general imitations of sonata-form are important only because they lead to certain imitations of the form of specific works. We find authors writing on symphonies and dividing their poems into movements, their movements into sections. Their works attempt at the same time to describe or interpret the music and to imitate its form. Later on we shall have occasion to analyze some of them. For the moment, suffice it to say that anyone attempting to describe a large work in any detail is likely to adopt its form, and that Frances Ridley Havergal, John Todhunter, and Richard Plattensteiner have written ambitious works of this type.

Often, however, poets fail to realize the importance of imitation of musical form, and are forced grotesquely to distort their accounts of music in order to fit them into a predetermined poetic form. The sonnet is particularly harmful in this way, as it is a form practically unknown in music, where a repetition of the octave after the sestet would be necessary in order to give a feeling of completion and satisfy accepted musical form. Mary Alice Vialls begins her sonnet, *Overture to "Tannhäuser,"*[46] with the Venusberg motif, neglecting the first third of the overture, and then proceeds to moralize over the defeat of the powers of evil:

> When lo! — as heaven's right to stern hell's wrong —
> Breaks in a solemn hymn that slowly swells,

etc. Her sonnet on a Chopin *Nocturne*[47] (Op. 37, No. 1) shows an even greater distortion of music for the sake of sonnet-form and morality:

> 'O wayfarers, say, whither are ye wending,
> By what laborious roads and pathways blind,
> Whereon your wearied feet the sharp stones find
> And thorns hedge all your course: whence is it tending,
> That toil-fraught path ye tread? 'Tis never-ending,
> Full chill upon it blows a deathly wind,
> Above its sterile waste shines no sun kind,

And over it an iron heaven is bending,'
So doth the music question, but it saith
Likewise: 'Bewildered souls who, straying, roam,
Hear yet the warning voice which calls you back
To the old fold; the master-key of faith
Alone will ope the gate that guides you home:
Seek it, and find again the ancient track.'

This sonnet would lead us to expect a first-section of somewhat harsh effect and strange harmony (the idea of seeking and the question "Whither?" are nearly always used to describe music of indefinite tonality or passages of dissonances extending to some length before resolution), followed by a surer, more conventional second section. Thus far, the poem agrees well with the music. The interpretation of the second section as a return to ancient faith is doubtless suggested by the direction *religiosamente* as well as by the use of four-part harmony in a hymn-tune effect. Musically, however, the piece cannot conclude with this section, and there is a return to the first theme, which this time has its contrast with the middle section even more strongly emphasized than before. The sonnet simply neglects this return: it will not fit the form of a sonnet, and, granted the interpretation which has been made up to this point, the music must be abandoned here or the moral will be reversed!

Our survey of the poets' attempts to imitate music shows that words invented for the purpose of reproducing musical sounds are really effective only for the percussion instruments, but that short passages using words carefully chosen for their sound can be highly suggestive of certain instruments. Even here, however, the imitation alone does not succeed, for the poet must guide us by telling what instruments he has in mind. Poetic rhythms are a more successful means of imitation, and a number of writers have used them tastefully and effectively, but many have neglected them, and even used them in defiance of the music under discussion. Poets who speak of harmony and counterpoint in poetry almost invariably mean something else, and the few genuine attempts at poetical counterpoint are merely grotesque. Musical form, however, from the echoing of a phrase to the extended use of a theme and variations, and even up to such complicated forms as fugue and sonata, has frequently been well used in verse to give something of the effect of a piece of music which the author wished to describe, although here, as elsewhere, we find many poets who have used strangely inappropriate forms. All in all, imitations of musical devices can be very helpful, but they can hardly be used alone to give the effect of music. We shall find that this is true for all the different elements used in attempts at poetic rendition of music, and that those poems which succeed best in this genre show a careful blending of imitation, description, and interpretation.

CHAPTER **III**

Description
of Music

In the preceding chapter the reader may have been surprised to find that, while certain poets appeared extremely sensitive to the formal elements of music and sought to reproduce them with the greatest possible exactitude, others seemed to have no regard for the most fundamental principles of rhythm and form, but freely violated both in their verses about music. One who has made any study of musical aesthetics will realize that this difference comes from the fact that there is no invariable way of listening to music. There are many different classes of auditors, and if we could make fine enough distinctions we should probably find that no two persons hear music in the same way. However, listeners fall into general classes, and some understanding of their differences is necessary for an investigation of their recorded reactions to music.

A number of studies of musical enjoyment have been made, and each authority groups his subjects in a different way, yet some broad generalizations are possible. Dr. Harry Porter Weld,[1] after a study of both mental and physiological reactions to music, grouped his subjects into three classes: (1) the analytic type, which hears music in a detached, intellectual way, seeking fully to grasp its structure and technique; (2) the motor type, which considers music in terms of actual or imagined movements; and (3) the imaginative type, which derives its enjoyment largely from the play of imagery drawn from the departments of the other senses, such imagery being called up by the music, though the music itself may be only on the fringe of consciousness.

43

Max Schoen[2] makes four general types. Subjects of the intra-subjective type lay the principal emphasis on the sensory or emotional effects which music has on them. With the associative type music is a means of arousing and stimulating associations with the past or visions which are probably the result of some sort of subconscious association. The objective type is what Weld called the analytic type; and the chief interest of the character type lies in characterizing the music as mystical, morbid, gay, playful, reckless, etc.

Vernon Lee[3] has made an extensive study of the variations in musical attention, using a large number of questionnaires sent out in various languages and answered by anyone who happened to be interested in the investigation. The answerers range all the way from conductors of symphony orchestras to people ignorant of the rudiments of musical notation, and thus the work probably includes everything of importance concerning the ways of hearing music. First of all, it makes a broad general distinction (a most important one for our purpose) between "listeners" and "hearers," who are found to be about equally numerous. "Listeners" are active and intellectual in their enjoyment of music. They are the class called "objective" and "analytic" by Schoen and Weld respectively. They have a good grasp of musical form and of the general principles of music, although they may not always have the technical terminology with which clearly to express their ideas. With them, listening to music is an occupation demanding intense concentration and undivided attention: if the music were to call up memories or suggest pictures these would be considered as disturbing factors interfering with the full enjoyment of the music itself. "Hearers," on the other hand, are largely passive; they may almost be said to "overhear" the music. They value it for the associations which it evokes, for the imagery which it suggests, for the moral allegories which they read into it, for the incidents in the life of an idealized composer which it leads them to invent — in fine, for everything except its specifically musical qualities. Since it is a stimulant rather than an end in itself, it need hardly be consciously heard. The extremists of this class prefer to keep a radio going in the corner while they read a novel or solve a mathematical problem. The "listeners" are a fairly consistent class, although it is quite likely that some pay more attention to rhythm, some to melody, some to form, etc. The "hearers," however, show any number of subdivisions, some of which were suggested above.

Interesting as they are, we cannot here attempt to classify them, but must be content with the occasional distinctions necessary for our purposes.

All three of our authorities on the classification of auditors are especially careful to state that there is perhaps no example of a pure type. The listener is likely to lose himself in visions and day-dreams if the piece he hears has not sufficient musical merit to hold his interest, and the musically uneducated man who would be a hearer at any symphony is likely to become a listener occasionally when he hears a piece of music so simple that he can easily grasp it. Nevertheless, in spite of an admixture of elements from all the varieties, most persons have a definite predominance of one type of musical attention.

In literature dealing with music the listener is a comparatively rare phenomenon, and the reasons for his rarity are obvious. In the first place, the impression given by an intellectual enjoyment of a composition is untranslatable: only a hearing of the music can give it. Lee finds that the listeners almost all testify to the existence of a *sui generis* musical emotion.[4] Also, though formal analysis can give a musician some idea of a composition, it seems to most authors to be absolutely unfitted for poetry, and when the pure listeners begin to write they more or less consciously abandon their customary point of view. "Hoffmann poète vaticinera sur la musique des sphères, mais musicien il goûtera autrement Mozart."[5] Most poets who write of music have something of the music of the spheres in their descriptions.

La musique reste prétexte à effusion lyrique: tantôt elle se confond avec l'amour, tantôt avec la religion, tantôt avec la nature, tantôt avec le mystère et l'au-delà: idée flottante, atmosphère trop vaste où tous les sentiments viennent baigner et pâlir. Voilà nos gens partis du havre musique pour un voyage d'association d'idées (qui d'ailleurs ont leur prix) sur la "Carte du Tendre" musical.[6]

Music remains a pretext for lyrical effusions. Sometimes it is confused with love, sometimes with religion, sometimes with nature, sometimes with mystery and the beyond — a hovering idea, a too vast atmosphere in which all sentiments float and fade. We can see our authors setting out from the haven of music for a voyage of associations of ideas (which have, for that matter, their own value) across the musical map of the Land of Love.

Nevertheless, we can recognize the intellectual musician, for he tells us in musical terms as much about the music as he dares, and then correlates his impressions and interpretations with the musical idea he has given us. The hearer often writes a poem on a symphony without once mentioning the music.

Hanslick summed up the creed of the musical absolutist in this matter when he wrote that specific musical devices have certain effects which they alone can produce:

Ein knapper oder weiter Rhythmus, diatonische oder chromatische Fort-schreitung, — alles hat seine charakteristische Physiognomie und besondere Art uns anzusprechen, darum wird es dem gebildeten Musiker eine ungleich deutlichere Vorstellung von dem Ausdruck eines ihm fremden Tonstückes geben, dass z. B. zuviel verminderte Septakkorde und Tremolo darin vorherr-schen, als die poetischeste Schilderung der Gefühlskrisen, welche der Referent dabei durch gemacht.[7]

A more restricted or broader rhythm, diatonic or chromatic progressions — everything has its peculiar physiognomy and its particular way of speaking to us. Therefore it will give a cultivated musician a far clearer impression of the effect of an unfamiliar composition if one tells him that, for example, there are too many diminished seventh chords and too much tremolo in it, than if one gives him even the most poetical account of the emotional crises which it produced in a listener.

A few musically trained poets, notably Browning, have taken this point of view and have treated music technically, to the great delight of musicians and the bewilderment of the general public.

Of all technical terms those dealing with harmony mean most to the musician and least to the layman, for a chord or a harmonic progression has a definite character of its own: the variety of rhythmical effects possible within, say, 4/4 time is almost infinite, but an authentic cadence, even with all possible voice-leadings, suspensions, and anticipations, always sounds like itself. Browning is particularly lavish in his harmonic descriptions. When he writes of an unidentified piece of music they serve to tell unmistakably the effect of which he wishes to speak, and when he writes of something which we know they keep its character constantly be-fore us. In *Abt Vogler* the conclusion of the master's extemporiza-tion is definitely described:

> Give me the keys. I feel for the common chord again,
> Sliding by semitones till I sink to the minor, — yes,
> And I blunt it into a ninth, and I stand on alien ground,
> Surveying awhile the heights I rolled from into the deep;
> Which, hark, I have dared and done, for my resting-place is found,
> The C Major of this life: so, now I will try to sleep.

This passage is so definite that one critic, although "treating the matter as a rather futile experiment," has written a passage of music to illustrate it.[8] "These six bars of commonplace may help some readers to attach a clearer meaning to the words," he writes. "My own feeling is that the verse is unworthy of a place in the poem." He is hard to satisfy, for he devotes pages to rather pedantic attacks on poets for their vagueness about music and their erroneous use of technical terms, but here, where he finds them both exact and correct, he still objects.

A Toccata of Galuppi's refers to "lesser thirds," "sixths diminished," and "commiserating sevenths," but its best use of harmony is the famous "Hark, the dominant's persistence till it must be answered to."[9] This clearly gives the idea of a dominant pedal-point progressing to the tonic. Here, however, we are still reading descriptions of unknown music, as in the generalized harmonic discussions in *Fifine at the Fair*.[10] In this last-named poem, however, we come to an attempt to describe some specific pieces of music. There is an extended passage[11] on Schumann's *Carnaval*, with especial reference to *Pantalon et Colombine*, in which the alternate staccato and legato passages are interpreted as the flight of Colombine from Pantalon. Here we find harmonic references in the mention of

> . . . the sweet monotony of those
> Three keys, flat, flat, and flat, and never a sharp at all.

Practically the whole of the *Carnaval* is in the keys of A flat, E flat, and B flat. (*Promenade* is in D flat, and several other pieces have sections in other keys using flats.) The complaint,

> or what if wrist were numb,
> And over-tense the muscle, abductor of the thumb,
> Taxed by those tenths' and twelfths' unconscionable stretch?

refers to the arpeggios in *Pantalon et Colombine* and the actual chords in *Eusebius*.

Parleyings with Charles Avison shows a more extensive and concrete use of musical terms than any other of Browning's poems. It speaks at length about a *Grand March* by Avison, which is used as the example in a discussion of change and fashions in musical taste. The manuscript of this piece was owned by Browning's father, and it is frequently printed at the end of the poem.[12] The technical discussion of the march, scattered throughout the poem, is here placed all together, with omissions indicated by asterisks:

* * *
                        No lure
Of novel modulation pricked the flat
Forthright persisting melody, — no hint
That discord, sound asleep beneath the flint,
Struck — might spring spark-like, claim due tit-for-tat,
Quenched in a concord.

* * *
                    Great John Relfe,
Master of mine, learned, redoubtable,
It little needed thy consummate skill
To fitly figure such a bass! The key
Was — should not memory play me false — well, C.
Ay, with the Greater Third, in Triple Time,
Three crotchets to a bar: no change, I grant,
Except from Tonic down to Dominant.

* * *
                    What, "stone-dead" were fools so rash
As style my Avison because he lacked
Modern appliance, spread out phrase unracked
By modulations fit to make each hair
Stiffen upon his wig? See there — and there!
I sprinkle my reactives, pitch broadcast
Discords and resolutions, turn aghast
Melody's easy-going, jostle law
With license, modulate (no Bach in awe)
Change enharmonically (Hudl to thank)
And lo, upstart the flamelets, — what was blank
Turns scarlet, purple, crimson! Straightway scanned
By eyes that like new lustre — Love once more
Yearns in the Largo, Hatred as before
Rages in the Rubato: e'en thy March
My Avison, which, sooth to say — (ne'er arch
Eyebrows in anger!) — timed, in Georgian years
The step precise of British Grenadiers
To such a nicety, — if score I crowd,
If rhythm I break, if beats I vary, — tap
At bar's off-starting turns true thunder-clap,
Ever the pace augmented till — what's here?
Titanic striding toward Olympus!

Here Browning speaks of all the musicians of past times who are
now dead, and then continues:

                            (Suit
Measure to subject, first — no marching on
Yet in thy bold C major, Avison,
As suited step a minute since: no: wait —

Into the minor key first modulate —
Gently with A, now — in the Lesser Third!)
                    *   *   *
                    Now —
Blare it forth, bold C major! Lift thy brow,
Man, the immortal, that wast never fooled.
                    *   *   *
                Therefore — bang the drums,
Blow the trumpets, Avison! March-motive? that's
Truth which endures resetting. Sharps and flats,
Lavish at need shall dance athwart thy score
When ophicleide and bombardon's uproar
Mate in the approaching trample, even now
Big in the distance — or my ears deceive —
Of federated England, fitly weave
March-music for the future!
                        Or suppose
Back, and not forward, transformation goes?
Once more some sable-stoled procession — say
From Little-ease to Tyburn — wends its way,
Out of the dungeon to the gallows-tree
Where heading, hacking, hanging is to be
Of half a dozen recusants — this day
Three hundred years ago! How duly drones
Elizabethan plain-song — dim antique
Grown clarion-clear the while I humbly wreak
A classic vengeance on thy March! It moans —
Larges and Longs and Breves displacing quite
Crotchet-and-quaver pertness — brushing bars
Aside and filling vacant sky with stars
Hidden till now that day return to night.

This poem has been quoted at some length because it exemplifies
practically all aspects of technical description. Browning takes
Avison's *March,* which is, he tells us, in C major and in ¾ time.
He gives an idea of its character by saying that it can be perfectly
harmonized with only two chords, the tonic and the dominant
(including the dominant seventh). He admits that modern taste
is inclined to call such a composition dull, but he undertakes to
show that it is the dress of music, not the fundamental idea, which
changes; he suggests that by means of harmonic complication and
rhythmic irregularities Avison's piece can be made to pass for a
modern work. When he speaks of dead artists he remarks, in passing, that, by modulating into the relative minor, we may use the
theme as a funeral march. He then writes the music of the future
with it, and after that suggests that Avison himself was once mod-

ern — his music can be archaized as well as modernized. The descriptions of music are absolutely essential to the poem. Browning has attempted to tell us enough about the methods he would use for putting this theme into various musical periods to enable us to imagine the effect, and unless we get this effect in each of the different forms of the theme we miss the fundamental idea of the poem: music has its fashions, but a single musical idea can appear again and again, under divers forms, so as to appeal to any age. Percy Grainger's transcriptions of folk-tunes and the jazz-bands' thefts from symphonic literature are living examples of Browning's suggestions about Avison's music.

It will be noticed that this poem has dealt with all the essential elements of music: scale-forms (major and minor, with perhaps a suggestion of atonality in the lavish sharps and flats of the music of the future), harmony, rhythm, and orchestration are all taken into consideration and described in more or less technical terms. Melody alone is little mentioned, and this for the obvious reason that the melody of Avison's *March* is taken as the constant idea amid all its changing accompaniments.

Other poems add only a few new elements in technical description. Occasionally technical phrases are taken directly from the score, as in Edgar Lee Masters' comment on the *Scherzo* of Beethoven's *Ninth Symphony:*

> The rhythm of three bars changed to the rhythm of four bars
> Is nothing less than the secret extasy of May.[13]

The movement is in $\frac{3}{4}$ time, *molto vivace,* and the score has the indication "Ritmo di tre battute" (bar 177), followed shortly by "Ritmo di quattro battute" (bar 234). Henry Van Dyke attempts a combination of imitation and description of rhythm when, in a poem entitled *Dance Music,*[14] he writes: "Smoothly it swings with a triplicate beat."

Jean Richepin calls attention to the simplicity of a sailors' song (printed at the head of the poem) when he speaks of

> Quelques couplets, naïfs de sens, veules de rime,
> Sur cinq notes, pas plus, cinq, mi, re, do, si, la.[15]

Some childish, weakly rhymed verses, on five notes — five, no more: E, D, C, B, A.

However, as a general rule, references to scale forms do not go beyond the obvious distinction between major and minor.

Harmony is more commonly mentioned, although even here the specific references seldom go beyond the distinction between consonances and dissonances — which are usually called "harmony" and "discord" respectively. Maurice Brillant's reference to the "précieuses dissonances" of Stravinsky[16] is both interesting and effective.

One of the most elaborate and skilful uses of technical harmony is that made by Richard Watson Gilder in his poem called *Music in Moonlight*.[17] He draws a moral lesson from the long-continued passages of dissonances in Schumann's *Mondnacht,* and learns

> The loveliness that from unloveliness
> Out-springs, flooding the soul with poignant joy,
> As the harmonious chords to harsh succeed,
> And the rapt spirit climbs through pain to bliss:
> Eternal question, answer infinite;
> As day to night replies; as light to shade;
> As summer to rough winter, death to life —
> Death not a closing, but an opening door;
> A deepened life, a prophecy fulfilled.
>   Not in the very present comes reply
> But in the flow of time. Should the song cease
> Too soon; ere yet the rooted answer blooms,
> Lo, what a pang of loss and dissonance!
> But time, with the resolving and intended tone
> Heals all, and makes all beautiful and right.
> Even so our mortal music-makers frame
> Their messages melodious to men;
> Even so the Eterne his mighty harmonies
> Fashions, supreme, of life, and fate, and time.

This may sound like a vague meditation on the laws of music in general, but a glance at Schumann's *Mondnacht* will show that it was carefully chosen as an example, and that Gilder had his eye on the object. A passage near the end of the song will illustrate this. Schumann has temporarily modulated to the key of F, which is here taken as the tonic, and the chords are as follows: I, V_7ii of VI, VI_7iii of F = II_7iii of C, V_7i, I, Ii, I, Ii, V_7iii, V_7i of IV (the voice ends on this chord, and the accompaniment continues), IV (with 4-3 suspension), IV, I. The accompaniment goes on for a few bars with its opening figure, and thus the song ends. These dissonances are of considerable duration, since the accompaniment is in slow eighth notes, and almost every chord has a full bar to itself; hence the general emphasis on dissonance is apt. But there is a more specific reference to this particular song in the words,

> Should the song cease
> Too soon, ere yet the rooted answer blooms,
> Lo, what a pang of loss and dissonance!,

for, as was noted above, since the vocal part stops on a first inversion of the dominant seventh chord of the submediant, the continuation of the accompaniment is absolutely essential.

We have seen that a poet cannot imitate the sounds of instruments, but he can easily describe orchestral effects by the simple process of mentioning the leading instruments and giving a general idea of what they are doing. To even the most unmusical person the names of a number of the commoner instruments will inevitably suggest their timbres, and poets dealing with orchestral music have taken full advantage of this fact. Plattensteiner uses it in various places to create a general impression of music when he is writing of pieces which he imagines, or at least does not identify. Thus, in *Kleines Orchester*[18] he writes:

> Es weben rings die Geigen
> Am wachsenden Tönemeer,
> Die Harfe gebietet Schweigen,
> Leise brummt,
> Eh er verstummt,
> Der Bass in der Tiefe:
> "Ich träume schwer."
> Hell das Horn ruft noch wach
> Manches geheime Weh und Ach.
> Sehnsuchtsvoll die Flöte erneut
> Erinnerung an das bisschen Freud'.
> Da — plötzlich mahnt der Geige fester Strich:
> "Vergiss nicht mich!"
> Doch die Flöte ruft: "Lass mich in Fried'!"
> Und singt es noch einmal, das holde Lied.

The fiddles weave a swelling sea of sound about us. The harp commands silence. Before becoming silent, the bass softly grumbles in the depths: "I'm having bad dreams." The horn sings out clearly and awakens many a secret pang. Longingly the flute renews the memory of a pittance of joy. Then — suddenly the firmer stroke of the violin warns: "Do not forget me!" But the flute cries: "Let me alone!" and sings its gentle song once again.

Sidney Lanier's *The Symphony*[19] has an identical use of instruments, combining a description of their performance with remarks read into their parts.

Descriptions of musical form can rarely be isolated, as they are usually more or less parenthetical remarks thrown in to keep the reader informed as to what point an author has reached in the interpretation of a work. Browning's description of a five-part fugue in *Master Hughues of Saxe-Gotha* has already been mentioned, and some attempts at imitating theme and variations and sonata-form also include incidental description of these forms. The description of a phrase and its answer as subject and answer is natural enough, and even technical terminology admits the analogy. Beethoven gave his sanction to this procedure when he wrote a question and answer for the subject and answer of the last movement of his *F Major Quartette* (Op. 135), heading the movement thus:

There is a good example of this commonplace in Nájera's *La Serenata de Schubert:*

> ¿No la ois como dice: "hasta mañana?"
>
> · · ·
>
> Y á la nota que dice: "¡hasta mañana!"
> El corazón responde: "¿quién lo sabe?"

> Don't you hear how it says, "Until tomorrow?"
>
> · · ·
>
> And to the note which says, "Until tomorrow!"
> The heart replies, "Who knows?"

Before entirely leaving technical description we must pause to call attention to the very interesting method of describing, not the music as it is heard, but the score itself. Browning used this technique in speaking of the modernizations and archaizations of Avison's *March:* "If score I crowd," "sharps and flats,/ Lavish at need shall dance athwart thy score," and "Larges and Longs and Breves displacing quite/ Crotchet-and-quaver pertness — brushing bars/ Aside" all refer to the score as seen rather than to the music as heard. For a musician they are probably more effective than a more extended description of the sound of the music could hope to be, for the scores of different periods and different composers have their own characteristic appearances which are alone sufficient to bring to mind the general effect of the music. Also, the score is far easier to describe than the sound. When Alice Meynell

wrote of the Bach prelude which Gounod took as an accompaniment for his *Ave Maria,* she said that "Bach led his notes up
through their delicate slope."[20] She was doubtless referring to the
appearance on the printed page rather than to any imagined slope
in the sound of the rising phrase.

The most remarkable use of this device is found in Edgar Lee
Masters' *Beethoven's Ninth Symphony and the King Cobra.* First
a jumbled account of the marks to be found on a score is given,
reminding one of some futuristic paintings, and having the same
purpose of giving a general impression of the subject. Anyone who
is accustomed to handling scores will have the idea of music in
general forcefully suggested by such a passage as this:

> It is more than a hundred years now since Beethoven
> Set down his misery and his ecstasy,
> His wounded and baffled spirit,
> His climbing and sun-lit and triumphant spirit
> In dots and curves, in numerals and time signatures,
> In key signatures, in breves and semi-breves,
> In major and minor keys, and ledger lines and clefs,
> In bars of duple, triple, and quadruple time, in rests and scales,
> In indications for winds and strings,
> Flutes, horns, bassoons and viols . . . .

A second passage describes the score in order to place more exactly
the compass involved in the descending jumps of the strings on
the dominant and tonic of the A triad:

> The second violins and cellos, the first violins, tenors and basses
> Begin to whisper their way from the top to the bottom of the treble stave
> To the bottom of the bass.

We have already remarked that the description of the change of
rhythm of the *Scherzo* in this poem was taken from the score, and
we shall find later that all the description and interpretation of
the music are borrowed from an analytical study of the symphony.

There are many attempts to tell what music does — to describe
it rather than to imitate it — which do not use technical language.
Here we begin to find attempts to translate music into words, and
it is only fair to remark that many of the poets who have attempted
this have themselves expressed doubt as to the legitimacy and possibility of such translation. A number of the poems on pieces of
music were doubtless written as experiments, although the fact
that several authors have written groups of such poems is proof
that they at least considered their experiments reasonably success-

ful. Even R. W. Gilder, one of the extensive writers of this type, had occasional misgivings, although he shows that they were transient when he names the poem in which he expresses them *A Mood*:[21]

> Words praising music, what are they but leaves
> Whirled round the fountain by the wind that grieves.
> Frail human speech falls idly as the snow
> On the red lava's flow, —
> Still pours the music on, all passion and flame;
> As music passes, that which music came, —
> Ever the same, with message never the same.

Jean Richepin is more hopeful when he attempts to describe an old sailors' song, *Les Trois Matelots de Groix*:[22]

> Comme dans un herbier les goëmons défunts
> Se dessèchent, flétris, et perdent leurs parfums,
> Cette musique et ces paroles, entendues
> Sur la mer qui frissone et dans les étendues,
> Vont-elles pas mourir et se flétrir aussi
> Sur ce froid papier blanc par ma plume noirci?
> Bah! les mots, vieux sorciers, ont des métempsychoses,
> Et leur philtres savants font revivre les choses.
> Essayons!

As the seaweeds in a botanical collection dry out, fade, and lose their perfume, will not this music and these words, heard on the broad expanse of the shivering sea, die and fade on this cold white paper which my pen blackens? Bah! words, old sorcerers that they are, understand transmigration of souls, and their occult philters make things live again. Let's make the attempt!

The results of this attempt certainly justified his hopes, but he had the advantage of dealing with vocal music and being thus able to use the text of his song for a good deal of the effect.

In the preface to *Neue Musikalische Gedichte* Plattensteiner takes up the same problem and gives his justification of the translation of music into verse.

Es ist vielleicht nur mehr eine Frage von wenigen Jahren, dass der Gehalt einer Tondichtung durch die Fortschritte der Wellenübertragung in Farben und in Worten zu uns sprechen wird. Bis dahin hat der Lyriker noch Zeit, zu versuchen, den geistigen Inhalt von Tondichtungen zu deuten und sich, gleich dem bildenden Künstler, ernstlich um diese Deutung zu bemühen. Manchen wird der Versuch als ein gewagtes oder gar als ein unmögliches Unterfangen erscheinen. Aber vielleicht dreht sich die Frage nicht darum, ob eine restlose und richtige Deutung aufscheinend wird, sondern vielmehr darum, dass — trotz der Armut der Sprache — ein Wortgebilde entsteht, das

im wesentlichen dem geistigen Inhalt von Tondichtungen näher zu kommen
sucht, aber keines, das nur Phantasie wäre.

It may be a matter of only a few years before the content of a musical composition, aided by the progress being made in the transposition of waves, will
come to us in the form of colors or words. Until that day the lyricist still has
an opportunity to attempt to interpret the spiritual content of musical compositions, and, as a creative artist, to apply himself seriously to this interpretation. Many will consider such an undertaking daring, if not impossible. But
perhaps the question is not whether a complete and correct interpretation
can be made, but rather whether (in spite of the poverty of speech) a poem
may arise which in its essentials attempts to approach the spiritual content
of the composition instead of being a mere fantasy.

We have already observed that Plattensteiner makes little attempt
at musical imitation, even in the most obvious matters of rhythm.
He does occasionally describe music, but this preface reveals
where his true interest lies: he seeks to give the "spiritual content" of music, and thus belongs to the school of the interpreters.
    John Todhunter is careful to state, at the beginning of his
collection of musical poems entitled *Sounds and Sweet Airs,* that

These poems are not meant to be paraphrases in verse of the music that suggested them. They are merely records of a listener's moods, phantasies inspired by the emotional spirit of each composition.

This general remark is true for a number of the poems, but there
are others which certainly are attempts at paraphrase. A "phantasy inspired by the emotional spirit of" Beethoven's *Sonata Appassionata* would hardly have a division into movements, with the
principal themes characterized, their entrances and combinations
noted, and the music described, sometimes bar by bar, along with
the interpretation — yet this is what we find in Todhunter's
poem.[23] The emotional spirit may have been his goal, but it is
certain that he often attempted to reach it by way of paraphrase.
    The general description of music offers little that is not already
familiar to any attentive reader of poetry; Keats is typical when
he speaks of "the music, yearning like a God in pain."[24] In the
field of harmony dissonances are still recognized, but are not often
mentioned as such. They are usually indicated by such words as
"seeking" or "yearning," and the strong tendency of a leading-tone
to its tonic, especially conspicuous in dissonances or suspensions,
is sufficient to explain the use of such terms. Occasionally it is
possible to recognize definite chords and passages. When Mary
Coles Carrington writes, in her poem on St.-Saëns' *Danse Macabre*:[25]

> (Twelve solemn strokes fell from the tower's chime.)
> "Aha, let's see!" — He harshly scraped the time,

the word *harshly* refers to the interval of the augmented fourth, double-stopped on open strings by the solo violin, and used, according to the program, to represent Death tuning his fiddle. More often we find a vaguer description of harmonies as "passionate," "wailing," "tender," "mighty," "tantalizing," "sonore," "effrayant," "languissant," "sourd," "hold," "hohl," "melodisch-donnernd," "süss."

Music in general is characterized in much the same way as harmonies, and such characterization requires little comment. It is often interesting to compare a poem with a score in an attempt to see what qualities or passages in the music suggested to the poet his description of it. Sometimes we find expressions which would seem to the casual reader to be mere commonplaces, but which prove to be particularly apt when we examine the music to which they are applied. Alice Meynell has several such phrases in her poem on Couperin's *Sœur Monique*,[26] as, for instance, when she speaks of

> This admired simplicity,
> Tender, with a serious wit.

The combination of seriousness, tenderness, and wit is even more clearly expressed in the lines,

> And if sad the music is,
> It is sad with mysteries
> Of a small immortal thing
> That the passing ages sing, —
> Simple music making mirth
> Of the dying and the birth
> Of the people of the earth.

And when R. W. Gilder tells of feeling his soul

> Slowly, irrevocably, and alone
> Enter the ultimate silence and the dark[27]

at the end of Tschaikowsky's *"Pathétique" Symphony,* he gives a felicitous description of the concluding bars of the work:

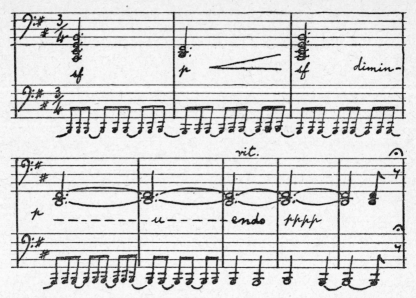

Certain generalizations may be made about this characterization of music. Even the most determined opponents of the theory that music is an expression of the emotions will admit that, since motion is one of its attributes, music can be described in terms of motion. Thus the terms "lively" and "tripping" are justified. So likewise are such words as "light" and "heavy"; they are accepted in this use, and it is only a step from them to "gay," "serious," "melancholy," and the whole host of other words attributing emotions and moods to music. All writers use such expressions, and they seem to agree reasonably well, or at least not to contradict each other, when two authors happen independently to describe the same composition. Nevertheless, it must be admitted that, since these descriptive terms cannot give any adequate idea of the music, the type of hearer who characterizes music cannot use this method very effectively for describing it to others. Anyone who has tried to identify the compositions alluded to in such poems as Gilder's *The Anger of Beethoven*,[28] in which we are told that

> — Sudden the music turned to anger, as nature's murmur
> Sometimes to anger turns, speaking in voice infuriate,
> Cruel, quick, implacable; inhuman, savage, resistless, —

realizes that, in spite of the six adjectives, it is impossible to guess with any degree of probability what composition the writer had in mind.

Description of music as motion is common enough for Dr. Weld to have grouped as one of his three classes of musical auditors those who hear and think of music in terms of real or imagined motion. The fact that music and poetry correspond in their development in time makes the description of a series of motions a reasonably effective way of describing music, although it is more effective still for recalling compositions which the reader already knows. Some of the best descriptions of contrapuntal music are given as accounts of the building of an edifice. Moritz Katz makes the figure stationary when he writes that

die Musik Bachs, Händels und anderer vielfach zur Vorstellung der Kirche führt und besonders die Bachsche Musik durch ihre scharfe Linienführung häufig den Eindruck *gotischer* Dome erweckt, obwohl dieser Komponist einer späteren Architekturperiode angehört.[29]

The music of such composers as Bach and Handel becomes a representation of the church, and the music of Bach especially, with its sharp sense of line, often gives the impression of a *Gothic* cathedral, even though Bach belongs to a later period of architecture.

The effect of motion is shown by comparing this statement with another passage which says, not that Bach's music is like a Gothic cathedral, but that the *performance* of his fugues is like the *building* of a great edifice. Bach's playing is being described:

> Er hämmert, fügt, er meisselt und behaut,
> Er mauert, und er zimmert,
> Gewaltige Balken über Balken baut
> Sich Stock- auf Stockwerk steil empor die Fuge.
> Dann klimmt an Sims und Zacke Lieblichflöte auf
> Und hängt den Richtkranz an den höchsten Knauf.[30]

He hammers, joins; he chisels and hews; he works at masonry and carpentry. The fugue builds itself up sheer, with great beams above beams, tier upon tier. Then the Lieblichflöte climbs up by cornice and crenellation, and hangs a garland on the highest peak.

In another passage[31] Lissauer describes a Bach suite in terms of the movements made in playing it, but this experiment is not so successful as the one quoted.

Many writers have attempted to describe music indirectly by describing the dance which it accompanied, but as a rule we know little about the music when the dance has been portrayed. Tennyson's "Come into the garden, Maud" is an example. When an actual performance of a dance is recorded, as in Grace Conkling's

La Argentina Dances: Fire Dance[32] and Albert Mérat's *Coppélia*,[33]
the effect can be striking and genuinely suggestive of the music,
but the innumerable long-robed funeral processions and dances of
village youths and maidens visualized by various writers while they
overheard pieces of music have nothing to distinguish them from
each other. Plattensteiner and Todhunter have numerous examples of these processions and dances. However, when they go
beyond the account of an actual dance which the author has seen
performed they become interpretation rather than description.

One of the commonest types of non-technical description is an
account of a performance of some piece of music. We are told, for
example, where it took place, who performed it, who was present,
and various other things as to the circumstances. Sometimes these
details simply set the stage for a description of the music itself,
but more often a knowledge of the music is assumed and the circumstances of the performance are a commentary on it. They may
easily be imaginary, but even if we have an account of some performance at which the author was actually present, if he merely
gives the setting and tells what was performed we can assume that
there is supposed to be some relationship. Were there no particular
significance in the setting, a poem describing it and merely mentioning the music would have no point whatsoever. Why should a
poet choose one out of the large number of musical renditions he
has doubtless heard unless it struck him as particularly significant? The use of music as a setting for love has been mentioned
before, and we find an excellent example of it, with some slight
description of the music, in Amy Levy's *Sinfonia Eroica*,[34] where
a performance of Beethoven's work gives the setting for a first
meeting of lovers.

The description of a performance, and especially of the audience, is most effective for satirical purposes. Franz Werfel's *Konzert
einer Klavierlehrerin*[35] is a masterpiece of this method.

> Die dicke Dame mit den Sommersprossen,
> Die tief sich in die Dekolletage wagen
> — Ich wünsche Blouse ihr und steifen Kragen —
> Sitzt schon am Flügel fett und hingegossen.
> Die Noten ziehn gleich schweissbedeckten Rossen.
> Chopin, der Trauermarsch — und so getragen —
> Ich fühle nur ein leeres Misbehagen,
> Von dieses Weibes Uebermass verdrossen.
> Die Schülerinnen sitzen in der Runde
> Und tun entzückt und hassen sie im Stillen.

Zehn Rosenkorbe glühn wie milde Fackeln
Aufleuchtend lieblich aus dem Hintergrunde,
Und schaun aus geängstigteń Pupillen
Auf ihre Brüste, die im Takte wackeln.

The heavy lady with the freckles which venture deep into her low-cut gown —
I wish she'd wear a blouse and a high collar — sits fat and overflowing at the
piano. The notes drag like sweaty horses. Chopin, the Funeral March — and
so labored — overwhelmed by this woman's bulk, I feel only an empty un-
easiness.

   Her pupils sit around her in a circle, and act delighted and secretly hate
her. Ten baskets of roses, like mild torches, glow cheerfully from the background and stare with a pained expression at her breasts, which waggle and
keep time.

We must know what was played in order to appreciate this poem.
The "schweissbedeckten Rossen" figure applies with particular
force to the march theme, and the irony lies in having such a work
performed thus and in such an atmosphere. Siegfried Sassoon has
two similar satirical poems, one of which describes North Oxford
getting culture at a performance of Bach's *B Minor Mass*.[36] The
other is a comment on the intellectual approach to Stravinsky
which, according to Sassoon, leads to a complete failure to understand *Le Sacre du Printemps*. For Sassoon the joke is that the
audience would be outraged if it were to grasp the meaning of
the music.

The Audience pricks an intellectual ear...
Stravinsky... Quite the Concert of the Year!
                    * * *

Bassoons begin... sonority envelops
Our auditory innocence; and brings
To Me, I must admit, some drift of things
Omnific, seminal, and adolescent.
Polyphony through dissonance develops
A serpent-conscious Eden, crude but pleasant;
While vibro-atmospheric copulations
With mezzo-forte mysteries of noise
Prelude Stravinsky's statement of the joys
That unify the monkeydom of nations.
This matter is most indelicate indeed!
Yet one perceives no symptom of stampede.
The Stalls remain unruffled: craniums gleam:
Swept by a storm of pizzicato chords,
Elaborate ladies reassure their lords
With lifting brows that signify "Supreme!"

> While orchestrated gallantry of goats
> Impugns the astigmatic programme-notes.
>
> But savagery pervades Me; I am frantic
> With corybantic rupturing of laws.

Sassoon goes on to describe the effect of the music on himself, i.e., what he considers its true meaning and intention.

The last part of this poem turns from a satirical account of the concert to a statement of the author's reaction to it. The practice of dealing with music by showing its effect on an auditor is frequently met with, but it is usually not particularly illuminating as to the music. Sometimes the emotions of a listener observed by the author are presented, and our only clue to the music is through an interpretation of the character of the auditor, as in Catherine Parmenter's *The Blue Danube*:[37]

> She stood there — puzzled — hesitant — before
> The little music shop. What sound was this
> That dared to mock her clever artifice,
> And swept — strange beauty! — through the open door?
> She could not understand this subtle thing —
> Who thought herself so altogether wise...
> Her flippant smile had fled — her hard young eyes
> Grew curiously warm and wondering.
> ...Oh, dreams of love, surging across the long,
> Long years to touch illimitable heights! —
> Starlight and dew of lost Vienna nights,
> Blent with the pulse of an eternal song! —
> The music ceased...Her laugh was swift and sure —
> But swifter still the tears that blinded her!

When the author deals with his own feeling he can hardly be said to write about the music at all, for the emotion described is more likely to be the final result of the composition than any accompaniment of it. Two of the best poems of this type will illustrate how little may be said of the music. Edna Millay's *On Hearing a Symphony of Beethoven*[38] is evidently supposed to be written while the music is in progress, but she does not specify to which symphony she refers, and the inferior first line, "Sweet sounds, oh, beautiful music, do not cease," is the only reference to the symphony as music. The remainder of the sonnet is taken up with music's unique power of bringing complete, even if temporary, happiness. Brentano's *Nachklänge Beethovenscher Musik*[39] shows by its title that it is not directly concerned with the musical work.

Finally, we come to the description of music by means of similes — a trick classified by Lee as "interpretation by 'as if.' "[40] In its most direct form this method compares to some familiar sound music which it has already attempted to describe in itself, and thus seeks to aid the reader's imagination. The comparison with singing birds is a poetic commonplace, and is frequently used to give the idea of an intermingling of themes. Thus Todhunter has

> The insistent march comes back, more dolorously sighing;
> And whirled along as in a storm
> The themes, like birds with songs changing their form
> To suit the season's weather,
> Now clamour all together,
> Now cry alternately alone,
> As joy and grief make antiphone.[41]

and

> Together now, now one the other leads,
> Like nightingales in May.[42]

So standard is this comparison that it is sometimes unthinkingly used, as in Masters' otherwise excellent description of the opening bars of Beethoven's *Ninth Symphony,* where he writes that "a clarinet breaks in like the call of a lonesome summer bird." This clarinet comes in *pianissimo* on the first beat of the fifth bar on an A, which it sustains into the fourteenth bar. It is barely audible. Hence the simile, poetic though it is to the reader, injures an excellent musical description, and would certainly give a false impression to a reader not familiar with the symphony. We shall hear more of this ornithophonic clarinet later.

More purely musical similes are to be found in attempts to define timbres. Thus Mérat has

> La musique s'égaie et raille vivement;
> On dirait, dans l'essor d'un caprice charmant,
> Les sons filés et fins des boîtes à musique.[43]

The music becomes lighter, with lively banter; by a charming flight of caprice one might call it the precise, thin sound of a music-box.

It is probably a carelessly handled simile of this sort which makes Todhunter startle his reader by the statement that, in Beethoven's *Sonata Appassionata,*

> With eager iterance flutter to the sky
> Notes from a preluding flute.[44]

This strange statement can be explained only as the assumption that he meant to compare the effect of these notes, after the heavy chords preceding them, to that of a flute. Comparisons to other musical sounds are common enough, and are usually helpful to the poet in his attempt to give some conception of the music which he discusses.

Natural sounds are often used (the birds are really more natural than musical), and they usually play some part in interpretation as well as in description. The words of *Long, Long Ago* were probably more influential than the music in Mörike's selection of similes:

> Es gibt ein altes Liebeslied, vom Norden kommt's,
> Wie ferne Glockenlaute, oder wie am Strand
> Eintönig sanfter Wellenschlag sich wiederholt,
> Dem man so gern, vergangner Zeiten denkend, lauscht;
> Denn endlos, süsser Wehmut unersättigt, kehrt
> Das immer gleiche Wort zurück: Lang, lang ist's her.[45]

There is an old love-song from the north, like the sound of distant bells, or the soft, monotonously repeated dash of waves on the beach to which we love to listen while dreaming of times long past; for endlessly, unwearied with sweet melancholy, the same phrase repeats: Long, long ago.

Jean Richepin's poem on *Les Trois Matelots de Groix* is particularly interesting from this point of view. He hears a fisherman in his boat singing the old song, and listens from the shore. At the end of each stanza there is a description of how it was sung. The first verse

> s'élance d'abord dans un vers répété
> Et là, sur un quasi trille qui pirouette,
> Plane en battant de l'aile ainsi qu'une alouette.

begins its flight with a repeated line, and then, pirouetting on a semi-trill, soars and beats its wings like a lark.

Henceforth the similes are all taken from the sea, and each one accords with the text of the stanza. In other words, the fisherman sings it feelingly, so that it sounds like a defiant laugh at the sea, like the north wind, and, finally, after the wreck:

> Ah! maintenant c'est comme un vol d'oiseaux meurtris
> Que la chanson là-bas se traine avec des cris.

Ah! Now the song over there drags itself along, crying, like a flight of wounded birds.

Still further removed from the actual music are similes which are purely imaginary, having nothing to do with sound at all. They differ from interpretation of music in terms of stories or scenes only in that the "as if" phrase is present. For example, if the quatrain

> Like wistful ghosts beneath a waning moon,
> Seeking a land they have no hope to find:
> Roving as homeless as a fitful wind,
> Faint notes arise and soft to silence swoon[46]

were to omit *like* (or substitute *pale*), we should have an ordinary specimen of visual interpretation of music.

We have seen that description of music takes various forms, more or less in accordance with the different types of musical auditors. Writers who speak of music in technical terms succeed in giving their readers fairly exact ideas of the music, but they become prosaic unless they mix a good deal of interpretation with their analyses. Descriptions of the score can be surprisingly effective, and they certainly give a clearer conception of the music than does the commoner practice of characterizing it by such adjectives as "stately" and "gay." Descriptions in terms of motion are more effective than any static attempts, although some of them are too commonplace to mean anything. Many poets give the setting of a concert or audition of a composition, and a contrast between the setting and the music is particularly effective for satirical purposes. The emotions of the hearer are sometimes a clue to the music, but more often they tell us nothing about it. Nevertheless, they remain a favorite subject of verse. Perhaps the most varied form of all is the simile. At one extreme of its many common uses is the clear presentation to the reader's mind of the sound under discussion; at the other are elaborate and often far-fetched visual interpretations. Like musical imitation, description alone cannot successfully recreate the writer's musical experience for his reader.

CHAPTER IV

Synaesthesia and the Confusion of the Arts

When a writer suppresses the term of comparison and says that music *is* a scene or a color, he may be either employing a literary metaphor or recording a conviction which to him is natural and inescapable. Let us take the ascription of color to music as an example. If we are told that music is green, it may mean that the writer has associations of green with this particular music — conscious associations coming from the color of scenery or lighting, from a performer's dress, or from any other accidental combination of the music and the color which happens to have impressed itself on his mind. It may mean that there is an intellectual analogy between the two — that he analytically recognizes certain similarities in the effect produced in himself by green and that produced by this particular composition. Finally, it may mean that there is an automatic and unreasoning equivalence between the two — that he has the impression of seeing green when he hears the music, but is unable to tell why. If this be the case the music will seem to him so obviously and necessarily green that he will probably wonder how anyone can question his statement. Here we have what is known as *synaesthesia,* the automatic interpretation of stimuli to one sense in terms of sensations of another.

This phenomenon has probably always existed to a certain extent, and the fact that its rudimentary form is present in almost every mind is shown by a study of language. The equivalence of such expressions as "loud colors," "couleurs criardes," and "schreiende Farben" indicates that there is a general tendency to feel bright colors in terms of loud or harsh sounds, and such common locutions as *hot* pepper, *soft* sounds, *warm* colors, and *sweet* music prove the universality of associations of sense impressions. However, in the nineteenth century a great development in the literary use of synaesthesia took place, and far more daring examples of it became literary commonplaces.

Louis-Bertrand Castel (1688-1757) went to some length in describing the possible construction of a "clavessin pour les yeux," and drew up a table giving the proper color for each tone of the chromatic scale.[1] He also suggested keyboard instruments for perfumes, and even for the senses of touch and taste.[2] Towards the end of the century various other writers commented, in a theoretical way, on the equivalence of the senses, and the associations between sound and color remained the central point of discussion. The advocates of colored hearing rested their claims largely on a proposition of Newton[3] showing that the intervals of our musical scale and the widths of colors of the spectrum are identical in their proportions.[4]

About the beginning of the nineteenth century the romanticists found that synaesthesia could be very effectively used to enrich their accounts of sensuous impressions, and since the exaltation of the senses was one of their prime objects, it came into general literary use, first in Germany, then in England (where Wordsworth, the first English poet to use it to any great extent, seems to have discovered it independently), and finally in France.[5]

The romanticists sought to combine all the senses. The fact that "Architecture is frozen music" has been attributed to Goethe, F. Schlegel, Schelling, and Görres, is alone sufficient to show how widespread such attempts were. The Aeolian harp — subject of so many romantic poems in German and English — was placed in flower beds in an attempt to secure a combination of perfume and music.[6] Hoffmann used all forms of synaesthesia extensively, and they became the common property of poets, although a few opposed the new technique. Thus Grillparzer says that Rossini has not been understood or appreciated:

> Den Meister aber kümmert's nicht.
> Er kennt die Welt. Mir deucht, er spricht:
> "Wenn sie mit den Augen hört,
> Mit den Ohren sieht,
> Mit dem Kopfe fühlt
> Und mit dem Gefühle denkt,
> Ist sie nicht wert, dass man sich kränkt."[7]

But this does not disturb the master. He knows the world. It seems to me that he says: "If the world hears with its eyes, sees with its ears, feels with its head, and thinks with its feelings, it is not worth bothering about."

The general confusion of the senses here described led to a confusion of the arts. If music can make things appear to the eye, it can paint; and if architecture can suggest harmonies to the ear, it can compose. Tieck suggested that pictures be accompanied by music, and most of the romanticists dreamed of a "Gesamtkunstwerk," later attempted by Wagner, in which all the arts should combine to produce a single effect.[8] The many interesting examples of confusion of the arts cannot here be discussed in detail.

In England synaesthesia was extensively used in poetry, but it never reached the importance that it had in Germany, or, later, in France, where it came to its full development about the middle of the nineteenth century. The Parnassians specialized in visual suggestion, and the symbolists in auditory, thus seeking to reproduce in their poetry the effects of painting and music respectively.[9] Baudelaire's famous sonnet, *Correspondances*,[10] sets forth the program of confusion of the arts followed by later French poets:

> La Nature est un temple où de vivants piliers
> Laissent parfois sortir de confuses paroles;
> L'homme y passe à travers des forêts de symboles
> Qui l'observent avec des regards familiers.
> Comme de longs échos qui de loin se confondent
> Dans une ténébreuse et profonde unité,
> Vaste comme la nuit et comme la clarté,
> Les parfums, les couleurs et les sons se répondent.
> Il est des parfums frais comme des chairs d'enfants,
> Doux comme les hautbois, verts comme les prairies,
> — Et d'autres, corrompus, riches et triomphants,
> Ayant l'expansion des choses infinies,
> Comme l'ambre, le musc, le benjoin et l'encens,
> Qui chantent les transports de l'esprit et des sens.

Nature is a temple in which living pillars sometimes emit confused words; there man passes through forests of symbols which watch him with familiar gaze. Like long, distant echoes which intermingle into a shadowy and profound unity, vast as night and brightness, perfumes, colors, and sounds correspond. There are perfumes fresh as the flesh of babies, sweet as oboes, green as the prairies — and others, which are corrupt, rich, and triumphant with the expanse of infinite things, such as ambergris, musk, benzoin, and incense, which sing the raptures of the mind and the senses.

Between 1871 and 1873 Rimbaud wrote a sonnet called *Voyelles*, beginning "A noir, E blanc, I rouge, U vert, O bleu, voyelles —," and setting out the characteristics of each according to its color. This colored hearing of vowels is probably the commonest phenomenon of genuine synaesthesia, and it has been frequently treated, both theoretically and literarily. Enough has been said of these transpositions of sense images to give a general idea of their prevalence, which has continued to the present day. Edith Sitwell uses them continually.

The one great objection to the literary use of the extreme forms of synaesthesia is that it conveys no definite idea to anyone but the writer himself. Those who have colored hearing cannot understand how anyone can fail to see the colors of sounds. Musset writes[11] "that he very much regretted having to argue with his family to prove that *fa* was yellow, *sol* red, a soprano voice blonde, a contralto voice brunette. He thought that these things went without saying." But the person devoid of colored hearing is comparatively fortunate, as these statements simply mean nothing to him. Those who have colored hearing have had furious arguments among themselves as to the colors of different sounds, and have never been able to agree. Thus René Ghil bitterly attacks Rimbaud's *Voyelles,* saying that Rimbaud must be a poser rather than one of the genuinely sensitive class to which, presumably, Ghil belongs.[12] According to Ghil, Rimbaud got the colors of the vowels wrong. Studies since that time have shown that there is no agreement at all in the colors ascribed to them, even among the most genuine cases of colored hearing.[13] However, even though Ghil's evidence was not admissible, his statement that Rimbaud was posing was a shrewd guess, and Rimbaud later admitted it. In *Une saison en enfer* he speaks of cultivating illusions of all kinds and inventing the colors of vowels: J'inventai la couleur des voyelles! — *A* noir, *E* blanc, *I* rouge, *O* bleu, *U* vert."[14] Even with this evidence we cannot be sure that the pose was entirely false. Millet tells of a number of cases of persons who, presumably desiring to be extremely "sensible," have developed colored hearing by suggestion *after* reading about it.[15] The complications which enter into any investigation of colored hearing are beautifully shown by Rimbaud's case. We already know that he first ascribed colors to the vowels and later admitted that the association was deliberately sought, but we can go beyond this. There is good evidence that the associations which he chose (whether conscious of their source or not it would be impossible to say) had been established in his early childhood. In *Voyelles* each vowel is connected with several words which begin with it, and these words are the names of objects which naturally suggest the color that Rimbaud ascribes to the vowel. It has been pointed out[16] that a children's alphabet-book current during Rimbaud's childhood is the obvious source for his associations. Each page of it had a large colored capital letter and four pictures of objects beginning with that letter. The colors of the vowels are those listed in Rimbaud's sonnet, and a number of the illustrative objects are the same.

Disagreements similar to that between Rimbaud and Ghil are common to all branches of synaesthesia except those rudimentary transpositions of sense impressions which have become accepted as a part of the language, and it is quite possible that these receive general acceptance only because they are learned almost in infancy, and are thus conditioned into agreement. References to the colors of music usually speak of the predominant instruments. but here, also, there is great confusion. A number of persons have assigned colors to parts of the orchestra, and a comparison of a few instruments, as described by a few writers, will show that the connection is entirely subjective. (See opposite page.)

We find a few minor points of agreement in this list. Instruments particularly rich in overtones, such as the horn, tend to be assigned shades requiring considerable mixture of the primary colors. Also, the same timbre becomes darker in color in the lower registers, as may be seen in Van Dyke's and Gardiner's colorings of the strings. The advocates of color-organs, having only an octave of colors, have similarly increased the luminosity of their colors with each ascending octave. Only one color is unanimously given, the bright red of the trumpet. However, we have here suggestion rather than independent agreement, for there is a famous story of Helmholtz to the effect that a blind man to whom someone was trying to describe the color scarlet said that he thought it must be like the sound of a trumpet. This story has been generally quoted, and several of the authors included in the table of instrumental colors mentioned it; hence the unanimity on this point.

The question of musical color is further complicated by the fact that not all observers take timbre as their criterion. For at least one woman it was the general character of a composer's work which gave his music its color, and the same composer would always have the same shade. She found Haydn an unpleasant green, Mozart blue in general, and Chopin largely yellow. This impres-

	VAN DYKE[17]	GIDE[18]	GARDINER[19]	GHIL[20]	LAVIGNAC[21]	HOFFMANN[22]	HUNEKER[23]	ORTMANN[24]
Oboe	green		yellow		green		green	rose-red
Flute			sky-blue	yellow	blue		blue	scarlet
English Horn	green				violet			
Clarinet		violet	orange		reddish brown	gold	purple	yellow
Bassoon	green	blue	deep yellow		dark brown		dark brown	violet
Horn	evening rose	rose	violet		yellow		glorious golden yellow	purple
Trumpet	red		scarlet	red	purplish red		red	red
Trombone	imperial purple	orange	deep red				scarlet	
Violin	noontide's hue	yellows & greens	pink	blue	variable	ultramarine	rainbow	ultramarine
Viola			rose				. . . .	
'Cello			red			indigo		indigo blue
Contrabass	ocean's hue		deep crimson red				hues	

sion of color was so strong that she had her scores bound in their proper tints.[25] Others have ascribed colors to chords or to various keys. Still others attribute them to different individual voices, and Arthur Upson has written *Quatrains of Seven Singing Ladies*,[26] in which he tells of hearing seven operas, mentioning who sang the part of which he speaks in each, and telling what color her voice was. Thus Lilli Lehmann as Isolde had a "sunsetred" [*sic*] voice, Schumann-Heink as Ortrude "blazed through the dark" in orange, while Emma Eames sang Elsa with a voice of violet.

All these variations make it impossible really to convey anything by the description of music in terms of color. Watts-Dunton begins his sonnet on Berlioz' *Damnation of Faust* as follows:[27]

> I had a dream of wizard harps of hell
> Beating through starry worlds a pulse of pain
> That held them shuddering in a fiery spell,
> Yea, spite of all their songs — a fell refrain
> Which, leaping from some red orchestral sun,
> Through constellations and through eyeless space
> Sought some pure core of bale —.

To what type of music does he refer when he speaks of "a fell refrain — leaping from some red orchestral sun"? His use of "a fiery spell" earlier in the poem, and the fact that he dreamt of "golden harps of earth" when he heard Gounod's *Faust,* and of "azure harps of heaven" when listening to Schumann's, may indicate that he chose red simply as the color of hell. But what would a casual reader think? On account of the accepted analogy between red and trumpets we might assume that it was played by the trumpets, but to Gardiner the color could equally well suggest trombones, 'cellos, or contrabasses. Others might think of red as being in a certain key: Musset would interpret it as music in the key of G, or perhaps over a pedal-point on G. Arthur Upson would imagine the "fell refrain" sung by Lilli Lehmann, and the lady of the colored scores might complain that it is all wrong because Berlioz' music is not red. Thus anyone who himself had some form of colored hearing would probably be misled, and to the vast majority of readers the lines would simply mean nothing. This difficulty besets all attempts to use synaesthesia in any specified way. However, it is possible to tell what the music actually is, and then to attribute colors to it in an effective way — effective, at least, for a reader who has not colored hearing, and hence will not dispute. A reader who heard music in terms of colors would probably consider this method worse than not describing the music at all, for it would make the description self-contradictory instead of merely misleading.

Colored hearing, though only one form of synaesthesia, is probably the commonest, and it is certainly the most important from our point of view. Other frequent interpretations of sound are in terms of light, the sun, moon, and stars, flame, shadows, water, plants, butterflies, and landscape.[28] However, common as these interpretations are among poets who describe music, it is probable that in most cases they are not genuine examples of synaesthesia, but are rather produced by associations with the music, or by a constant search for and interpretation of sounds which may be considered as imitative. Frequently synaesthesia and musical suggestion are inextricably entangled, as in some of the descriptions of dances and processions, where the idea of motion certainly comes from observation of musical rhythms, but the colors of robes and dresses may easily be due to some form of colored hearing.

The general tendency towards confusion of the arts which accompanied the literary development of synaesthesia is shown in a number of poems. In the first place, any poem which seeks to reproduce the effects of music in any way is in itself an example of this confusion; almost any of the poems which have been quoted thus far will serve as illustrations of this fact. Moreover, the poems, which are in themselves confusions of the arts, often carefully develop further confusions in their subject matter. Music may be described in terms of painting or poetry, and the verses, as we have seen, often have names and directions for reading which are borrowed from music. One of the commonest and most effective of these combinations is that of music and architecture. Its frequency may be explained partly by certain similarities between these arts, and partly by the influence of the famous aphorism that "Architecture is frozen music." A description of a Bach fugue in architectural terms has already been quoted, and is an excellent example of the lengths to which the confusion of the arts has been carried: it is an attempt in a poem to recreate the effect of music by a use of architectural images. The Frenchman who, in praising a poem, exclaimed, "C'est de l'exquise musique peinte!",[29] went no further.

Not all recorded cases of synaesthesia can be believed, and not all confusions of the arts are sincere attempts at self-expression; hence we must proceed with some caution in accepting them. We know that Rimbaud's colors for the vowels were not unpremeditated, even though the association had been set up in his mind years before. It would be difficult to disprove a person's claim to have colored hearing, and, in view of the popularity of this phenomenon among the professionally sensitive during the last century, it is probable that there were more than a few false pretenders to the honor. The fact that, in most cases, the subject does not actually *see* a color, but merely has an impression of it, would make it easier to deceive both oneself and others. Erika von Siebold found that the examples of synaesthesia used in poetry do not always correspond with the poet's own experiences, as noted in letters and diaries,[30] and whether we consider this fact as evidence of charlatanry or of use of the poetic imagination, it is certainly proof that not all the literary uses of synaesthesia and kindred phenomena can be accepted as records of fact.

Similarly, in the confusion of the arts there is a good deal of insincere "fine writing." In supposedly aesthetic studies we find such passages as this:[31]

Toute forme d'art est musicale, si elle est vraiment artistique. L'architecture est une musique dans l'espace. La poésie est une musique de la pensée en passion avec la vie. Et Psyché le sait bien, qui se donne éternellement à l'Amour, pour que naisse le chant.

La musique est la poésie de Psyché qui s'éveille. La musique trompe l'ombre, et elle enchante les ténèbres.

La musique est le soleil du crépuscule.

La musique est le soleil et le miroir de la tristesse.

O chant, c'est toi l'invitation à l'oubli.

Every form of art is musical, if it is really artistic. Architecture is a music in space. Poetry is a music of thought in its passion for life. And Psyche knows this well, she who eternally gives herself to Love, so that song may be born.

Music is the poetry of Psyche awakening. Music deceives the shade and enchants the shadows.

Music is the sun of twilight.

Music is the sun and the mirror of sorrow.

O song, thou art the invitation to forgetfulness.

This may have been written seriously and in good faith, but the reader is certainly privileged to suspect it of being meaningless affectation. The desire to seem both sensitive and original often leads to the writing of utterly absurd interpretations of music:

Die Meistersinger is a musical rose-thicket alive with passionate golden-throated bulbuls and merry velvet butterflies; it has the perfumed beauty of some sunny Persian paradise whose sinuous tigers are adorable purring pussy-

cats. I see in the *Preislied* an enchanted crimson rose that sheds its shining
petals over the whole opera [. . .], and in those subtler songs entrusted
to the cobbler a cluster of ruby-hearted buds of a more penetrating sweetness.
This music is all rose colored, with gleams of sunny gold . . . .[32]

However, when all allowance has been made for insincerity, the
fact remains that colored hearing is a reasonably common phenomenon, and that a number of outstanding musicians and men of
letters, including Liszt, Meyerbeer, and Wagner, are known to
have had it to a greater or less degree.[33] Many theories have been
invented to account for it,[34] but only two need concern us here.
According to one of these, all forms of synaesthesia come from previously conditioned associations of ideas, and thus they differ from
the ordinary method of dealing with music in terms of the memories it evokes only in that the poet is unconscious of the connection
between the music and the colors, scenes, or stories which it suggests to him. The other theory is that of mental equivalence. According to it, the music never directly suggests anything else, but
rather produces a state of mind which, in turn, suggests something
which might produce or which has produced the same mental state.
According to the first of these theories, the music and the elements
which enter into its interpretation are connected in the mind by
some past simultaneity, whereas the second connects them by a
similarity in their effects on the auditor. The fact that some persons remember music, not as sound, but as a series of emotions,[35]
tends to support the second theory, which Percy Scholes has summed up very simply and directly:[36]

The fact is, I think that music can arouse emotions and that colours can do
the same, and that what connection there is between music and colour is not
physical and direct, but subjective and viâ emotion. This does not apply to
key (except in the case where key has for a particular observer a fanciful
emotional significance of its own). But it does apply to timbre and also to
the general character of a passage (rhythm probably often entering as a
factor). A trumpet fanfare suggests joy: red to me suggests joy; hence a
trumpet fanfare to me suggests red. That is my idea of the matter.

The association of extraneous ideas with music, often indistin-
guishable from synaesthesia, is an extremely common phenomenon
and a favorite subject of poets. It usually takes the form of comments on the power of music to remind the listener of the circumstances under which he has formerly heard it, and a number of
poems have been devoted to this theme. Cowper treats it in a
typical fashion:

How soft the music of those village bells
Falling at intervals upon the ear
In cadence sweet! Now dying all away,
Now pealing loud again, and louder still,
Clear and sonorous, as the gale comes on.
With easy force it opens all the cells
Where memory slept. Wherever I have heard
A kindred melody, the scene recurs,
And with it all its pleasures and its pains.
Such comprehensive views the spirit takes,
That in a few short moments I retrace
(As in a map the voyager his course)
The windings of my way through many years.[37]

Ricarda Huch,[38] Walter Savage Landor,[39] and many other poets
have written similar praises of the evocative power of music, and
Celia Thaxter has an interesting poem telling of a performance
of Schumann's *Sonata in A Minor* in a room full of poppies in the
summer. She rejoices that a mental association has been set up
whereby even in winter this music can bring back the feeling of
summer:[40]

But winter cannot rob the music so!
Nor time nor fate its subtle power destroy
To bring again the summer's dear caress,
To wake the heart to youth's unreasoning joy, —
Sound, color, perfume, love, to warm and bless,
The airs of balm from Paradise that blow.

It will be noticed that part of the power to evoke this scene in the
future is attributed to the music itself, and that it is supposed to
recall color and perfume in a manner typical of cases of supposed
synaesthesia. Were the author to begin at the other end, with a
subsequent performance of the sonata, and inform us that it was
scarlet music, we should have no way of knowing the poppy association, and should regard it as a case of colored hearing.

In the two following extracts on *Taps* we probably have association rather than true synaesthesia:

Into pure night
A strand of golden sound
Weaves a design,[41]

and, similarly,

— Come notes of a bugle —
Mincing, silver-slippered steps of music.[42]

The writers of these lines are thinking of the instrument and associating the sound with it: the two colors given to its tone are the two colors which a bugle — in the pre-plastic age — could be.

As we saw in Celia Thaxter's poem, even a single performance, if it be sufficiently impressive, can set up an association, but the habitual connection between a composition and any external object or idea is far stronger. (This fact is used to good advantage in the Wagnerian Leitmotiv, which employs such associations to attach a special significance to a short, easily remembered musical phrase.) In general, it seems that the less specifically musical interest and comprehension a listener has, the more he tends to connect music with the external accidents of its performance. Poets of this type are prone to attach a sentimental value to a song because of some woman who used to sing it, and this approach is common from Ronsard to Gérard de Nerval, and on down to the present day. More interesting examples are to be found in music which has not been used with the composer's original intention, and has thus acquired for the popular mind a purely accidental significance. Handel's *Largo* has been so often played by church organists that it is invariably taken as an expression of Christian piety and praise, as in Gilder's sonnet,[43] which begins:

> When the great organs, answering each to each,
> Joined with the violin's celestial speech,
> Then did it seem that all the heavenly host
> Gave praise to Father, Son, and Holy Ghost.

and continues in the same vein. In its original form in the opera *Xerxes,* the *Largo* is merely a tenor aria in doggerel praise of the grateful shade of a palm tree.

When words are sung with the music (as spurious ones sometimes are with the *Largo*) the association becomes still more powerful. It has been necessary to examine accounts of vocal music very carefully before admitting them to the discussion in this study, and they have been as far as possible avoided for the reason that they usually take their central idea from the text rather than from the music. In the case of opera, poets are even likely to abandon both words and music in order to deal with either the plot or the stage-business. Writers who have made programs for Beethoven's *Ninth Symphony* plunge into the finale with an almost audible sigh of relief, for at last they have a text on which to hang their interpretations. Handel offers one of the most interesting examples of how far the mind will go in assuming that the words commonly heard with a piece of music are a complete expression of its meaning. He never scrupled to lift material from other composers or from himself, and the remarkable speed with which he composed *Messiah* was at least partly due to this habit. A good deal of the music of the oratorio is taken over bodily from Italian love-songs which he had already composed, some a few months earlier and some as far back as thirty years. Since *Messiah* is still widely performed and the songs are forgotten, listeners assume that the music of such numbers as "For unto us a Child is born," "And He shall purify," "His yoke is easy," "All we like sheep have gone astray," and "O death, where is thy sting?" somehow express the religious ideas of the words and were, in fact, written as a response to them. A glance at the trivial doggerel of the texts for which this music was originally composed will give a salutary shock to one's preconceptions about the power of music to convey non-musical concepts.[44] It will also explain certain traits of the music as now performed. For example, the melisma on *easy* (in "His yoke is easy") can be explained only by the fact that the word was originally *laughs* (Italian *ride*), and the passage was written to illustrate the flower laughing in the light of dawn.

Similar examples could be cited from Bach and Gluck, but enough has been said to show that the interpretation or description of vocal music usually has little to do with the music. Some of the interpretations of instrumental music are equally remote, but at least they are written in response to the music, whereas those who write of vocal works confine themselves, as a rule, to the words. Hence we shall omit them from our discussion except when they unmistakably refer to the music itself, as was the case in Gilder's poem on Schumann's *Mondnacht*.

As an example of the ease with which associations between even the most dissimilar things may be formed, we may take the confession of so good a musician as Grillparzer. In his diary for 1822 he recollects that, as a child, he studied the violin-and-piano sonata of his teacher, Gallus, while he was reading a thriller of that time called *Der schwarze Ritter*. By an association of ideas he reached the point where either of these works suggested the other, and the sonata, which was "nichts weniger als düster oder heftig, vielmehr sehr lieblich," seemed horrible to him and always called up images of terror.[45] Had Grillparzer had a bad memory he might have forgotten *Der schwarze Ritter* and, throughout the rest of his life, insisted that there was something horrible in the music of the sonata, or that it was an expression of terror.

Closely related to association, and an equally powerful force in producing strange interpretations of music, is verbal suggestion. A descriptive title given to a composition is a sufficient guarantee that all "hearers" will interpret it in accordance with the title, even if, as in the case of Beethoven's *"Moonlight" Sonata,* that title is a later invention unsanctioned by the composer. There are several amusing instances of the suggestive power of an erroneous title.

George Sand furnishes a good example. In her *Lettres d'un voyageur* there are two passages[46] of ecstatic comment on the power of Beethoven's *Pastoral Symphony* to evoke landscape. The first of these states that hearing the music has often enabled her to re-experience the landscape of Italy. The second begins with a statement that except for metaphysical dissertation (an exception not to be regretted) music can express everything: Beethoven's symphony is not so exact as a landscape painting, but it calls up all the beauties of natural scenery, including illimitable horizons, storms, songs of birds, sunlight, and, finally, a state in which the listener loses his personal identity and becomes a part of nature. Unfortunately, between these two passages George Sand gives the following anecdote as an illustration of the nature of music:

C'est le champ le plus vaste et le plus libre qui soit ouvert à l'imagination, et, bien plus que le peintre, le musicien créé pour les autres des effets opposés à ceux qu'il a créés pour lui. La première fois que j'ai entendu la symphonie pastorale de Beethoven, je n'étais pas averti du sujet, et j'ai composé dans ma tête un poëme dans le goût de Milton sur cette adorable harmonie. J'avais placé la chute de l'ange rebelle et son dernier cri vers le ciel, précisément à l'endroit où le compositeur fait chanter la caille et le rossignol. Quand j'ai su que je m'étais trompé, j'ai recommencé mon poëme à la seconde audition, et il s'est trouvé dans le goût de Gessner, sans que mon esprit fît la moindre résistance à l'impression que Beethoven avait eu dessein de lui donner.[47]

It is the vastest and freest field open to the imagination, and, much more than the painter, the musician creates for others effects different from those which he has created for himself. The first time I heard Beethoven's *Pastoral Symphony* I was not aware of the program, and I made up, in my own head, a poem in the style of Milton to interpret that delightful harmony. I placed the fall of the rebel angel and his last cry towards heaven precisely at the point where the composer introduces the songs of the quail and nightingale. When I learned that I was wrong I began my poem all over again at a second hearing, and this time it was in the manner of Gessner, without my mind's making the slightest resistance to the impression which Beethoven had intended to create.

It would be hard to find a better illustration of both the failure of untitled music to control a hearer's programmatic responses and the ease with which these responses can be controlled by a verbal indication of the composer's intention. But similar incidents might be multiplied almost indefinitely. The general conclusion is clear: whenever music bears some sort of descriptive title interpreters are sure to take this into account and to agree with each other *in so far as the title can control their ideas*. As soon as they pass beyond its explicit control, however, they reveal all the differences and contradictions characteristic of interpretations of music in terms of anything except itself.

Words play a large part in all thought, and are probably responsible for a great part of the translation of music into verbal concepts, particularly when such translation takes the form of moral allegory. Most of these verbal connections with music are so obscure as to defy analysis unless we have a detailed knowledge of the auditor and of all the circumstances. Vernon Lee gives a brilliant analysis[48] of one case, showing how such interpretations may be formed. She discovers the logical steps by which word association, combined with a number of other elements, led one person regularly to connect the *Fidelio Overture* with a Swedish story of the death of a horse, and even to identify the horse with Beethoven. However, it is only rarely that we have sufficient information for an analysis of this kind. As a rule, we must take interpretations of music in terms of pictures or stories as they come to us, without being able to tell how they were formed.

In conclusion, we may say that description of music as color or any other non-auditory impression can tell us nothing about the music, and to those who are themselves inclined to describe music in this way it is almost sure to be misleading. Nevertheless, it may be well used for vague musical effects, or it may be effectively combined with some description of the music *per se*. In general, synaesthesia has been much abused, and is to be received with some suspicion. In poems dealing with music it is often difficult to distinguish between synaesthesia and simple interpretation, since the two are often thoroughly entangled. The translation of sound into other sensations naturally leads to the confusion of the arts which is often found in poems dealing with music. Poetry cannot well describe music in terms of poetry, and the other arts are all static.

Hence the best efforts at presenting music in terms of the other arts have compared the performance of music to the original construction of works in the visual arts, thus securing the effect of movement combined with structural development which is absolutely essential in music. Architecture is probably used in this way more frequently than any other art, and, with skilful handling, this method can produce excellent results. On the whole, however, synaesthesia and the confusion of the arts have probably injured the treatment of music in poetry more than they have aided it.

The associations which are probably the cause of synaesthesia also manifest themselves in various other ways, the simplest and commonest being an evocation of memories. Word association and various other elements also enter in, usually in obscure and complicated relationships, and it is probably true that all interpretation is ultimately based on some form of association.

CHAPTER V

Visual Interpretations of Music

Towards the beginning of this century a book was printed which stated that "A song is, or ought to be, a picture. We often hear songs, and playing too, which call before us no picture. What an art failure!"[1] These pictures are the stock in trade of the visual interpreters of music, who set out to explain them to those who cannot see them at all, or to those of their own group who see different ones. On the other hand, only a few months ago Aaron Copland polished off this sort of interpretation, even when done by the composer himself, with the forthright dictum, "If you have to explain it, the hell with it."[2]

There are many possible compromises between these two extreme views, and probably few persons would agree entirely with either, but there is a large body of "hearers" who would tend towards the former. This type has always had a tendency to interpret music in terms of pictures and stories, and the great increase in avowed program music during the last century was certainly an encouragement to such interpretation. Even when no program or suggestive title was given with the music, writers who enjoyed translating music into other terms said that composers had doubtless had programs in mind at the time of writing, but had not seen fit to publish them.[3] Such authors are inclined to view the scene or picture which they derive from a composition as its real purpose, and to consider that the only true understanding of a composer is a perception of the pictures which he is thought to have had in his mind's eye when composing. They frequently assert that these pictures can be arrived at with reasonable certainty.

82

There are various musical elements which, according to the advocates of descriptive music, can be used to give the correct and unique meaning of a composition. Edward MacDowell's essay on *Suggestion in Music*[4] discusses these devices. After dismissing form and the intellectual appeal of music as relatively unimportant, he says that the repetition, recurrence, and periodicity of sound can bring up definite ideas, as can the mere imitation of natural sounds. "The songs of birds, the sound made by galloping horses' feet, the moaning of the wind, etc., are all things which are part and parcel of the musical vocabulary, intelligible alike to people of every nationality." Patterns (such as the traditional spinning-wheel one) and pitch are effective. Harmony has a strong suggestive power: for example, avoidance of the primary triads and the extensive use of chords from foreign keys give a feeling of mystery. In modern music, tone-color is also greatly used for suggestion.

The suggestive power of all these devices is undeniable, but MacDowell and many others make extravagant claims for them. A comparison of interpretations of the same music, written by different persons without the assistance of program notes or a descriptive title, will prove conclusively that it is beyond the power of music to communicate any single scene or story to its auditors. Even the most obvious of all methods, the direct imitation of natural sounds, cannot produce unity of interpretation. In an experimental study Voelker's *Hunt in the Black Forest* was played to a number of persons (the title being, of course, suppressed), and they wrote their interpretations of it. The conclusions reached by this experiment were as follows:[5]

A survey of these introspections reveals an enormous individual variation in the mental contents of several auditors. It is true that several of the introspective descriptions contain elements in common: an outdoor scene; songs of birds; animals; the dawning day; rapid and vigorous action, and the like; but the setting or story into which these elements are interwoven shows a marked difference from individual to individual. One auditor conceived the music to be a portrayal of a battle; another, of a circus; another, of a melodrama; another, of a hunting scene. It is a remarkable fact that even the purely mimetic descriptions, such as the barking of dogs, wholly failed in certain instances to arouse situations such as the composer and conductor had hoped to simulate. [. . .] These introspections show that the composer is powerless to evoke any one definite mental picture in the minds of all his auditors.

It should be added that one of the best musicians among the subjects of this experiment heard everything as thematic material and failed to notice some of the most direct imitations of natural sounds. Experiments such as this flatly contradict MacDowell's statement about imitative sounds "intelligible alike to people of every nationality."

However, it would seem that certain vague emotional states are more easily conveyed by music than are external objects. Nearly all the interpreters of Beethoven's *Ninth Symphony* have found the opening of the first movement mysterious or vague (it is frequently interpreted as a representation of chaos), and this effect is due to a harmonic device of the type mentioned by MacDowell. Beethoven avoids the mediant, and thus makes the tonality indefinite. We see, then, that it is difficult to represent in music any particular scene so that the auditor will divine it without the aid of a suggestive title or note. The representation of vague feelings and moods is easier, but even here opinions on compositions are far from unanimous, and the attempt to define these feelings in words often leads to confusion.

A further point in connection with this visual imagery is that it is involuntary: the subject simply hears the music and sees visions simultaneously, without any effort of the imagination.[6] However, since many listeners derive their chief pleasure from the play of imagery suggested by the music, it is likely that they consciously attempt to keep the imagination active and thus to make this imagery as varied and entertaining as possible. Mme. Edgar Quinet gives an interesting series of her interpretations of Beethoven's *Ninth*[7] through a number of hearings, and in these we find that her ideas crystallize and become more definite with each successive hearing. Entirely new elements also enter into her interpretation from time to time, and then reappear regularly in subsequent introspections. The recording of such a series of impressions probably indicates a certain conscious effort towards formulating a complete and coherent interpretation of the symphony.

We cannot assume that all poets who deal with music in terms of visual imagery actually have the involuntary visions described by Weld. A person of the motor type often listens with real motions accompanying the music, or he may imagine such motions, and in the latter case he will probably see dances, battles, races, etc., at the time of hearing the music. Other listeners simply use visual imagery as a convenient way of describing music to a third party. The answerers to Vernon Lee's questionnaires make this point clear. "Music doesn't make visual images at the time," writes one, "but in retrospect. — It would be in describing that I might think of as crowds what I felt as hurry and conflict; [describe] as processions, armies, what I felt as dignity, energy, peace, resignation."[8] Another goes even further: "The imagery used in describing music to a third person is a more or less conscious imposture."[9] As we shall see, it is also a very ineffective imposture.

If music cannot produce the same vision in different auditors it is obvious that a verbal description of one of these varying visions can never give anyone not familiar with the music which it attempts to portray any idea of the nature of that music. We may quote two poems on Chopin's *Fifteenth Prelude* to illustrate a number of points about the description of music in terms of scenes. The first, by Philip Bourke Marston, is called *The River (Suggested by the Fifteenth Prelude of Chopin)*:[10]

> The river flows forever —
> The moon upon it shines —
> One walks beside the river
> With heart that longs and pines.
>
> A breeze moves on the river,
> The moon shakes in its flow —
> He grieves and grieves forever,
> For days of long ago.
>
> The softly lapping river,
> It whispers in its flow
> Of dear days gone forever,
> Those days of long ago.
>
> He listens to the river,
> A spirit seems to say —
> "Forever, Love, forever,
> Some day, some blessed day!"
>
> Between the moon and river
> The spirit seems to glide —
> He cries — "To-night, forever,
> I'll clasp thee, O my bride!"
>
> And the happy pilgrim river,
> As it journeys to the sea,
> Sings, "Ever and forever,
> Together they shall be!"

The second, by Robert Underwood Johnson, is entitled *A Chopin Fantasy*:[11]

Come, love, sit here and let us leave awhile
This custom-laden world for warmer lands
Where, 'neath the silken net of afternoon,
Leisure is duty and dread care a dream.
                    (*The music begins*)
That cliff's Minorca, that horizon Spain,
There in the west, like fragrance visible,
Rises the soft light as the sun goes down
Till half the sky is palpitant with gold.
Follow it eastward to the gentle blue,
With faith and childhood in it, and the peace
Men agonize and roam for. See that fleet
That flutters in the breeze from the Camargue
Like white doves, huddled now, now scattering.
(They say all native boats are homeward bound
Against tomorrow's annual festival.)
What peace there is in looking from this height
On palms and olives, and the easy steps
By which the terrace clambers yonder hill!
How dark those hollows whence the roads of white
Ascend in angles to the high-perched town!
Needless the music of the convent bell:
'Tis vespers in the heart as in the air.
This is the hour for love, that, like the breath
Of yonder orange, sweetness is at eve.
Here, safe entwined, what could be wished for two
Hid in an island hidden by the sea?
Now let me lay my head upon your lap,
And place your rose-leaf fingers on my lids,
Lest, catching glimpse of your resplendent eyes,
My ardor should blaspheme the coming stars!

    .   .   .   .

How fast it darkens! One must needs be blind
To know the twilight softness of your voice.
And Love, — not blind, but with a curtained sight, —
Like one who dwells with Sorrow, can discern
The shading of a shadow in a tone.
There's something troubles you, my sweet-of-hearts,
A hesitance in that caressing word;
Nothing unhappy — a presentiment
Such as from far might thrill the under-depths
Of some still tranquil lake before a storm.
Be happy, love, not ponder happiness.
Unerringly I know your woman's soul,
Content to have your happiness put off
Like well-planned feast against tomorrow's need,
And more enjoyed in planning than in use.
But oh, we men, God made us — what was that?

A drop upon your hand? Perhaps a tear
Lost by an angel who remembers yet
Some perfect moment of th' imperfect world,
And goes reluctantly her way to heaven,
Still envious of our lot? Another drop?
Why, 'tis the rain. Stand here and see that sky —
Blackness intense as sunlight. What a chasm
Of silver where that lightning tore its way!
That crash was nearer! Here's our shelter — quick!
Now it's upon us! Half a breath, and — there!
No wonder you should tremble when the earth
Sways thus, and all the firmament's a-reel.
Tremble, but fear not — Love created Fear
To drive men back to Love, where you are now.
What rhythmic terror in the tideless sea
That wildly seeks the refuge of the rocks
From unknown dangers (dangers known are none)!
God! Did you see whiting the headland's jaws
That drifting sail? Wait the next flash and — look!
Oh, heaven! To cruise about a hundred coasts,
Safe past the fabled monsters of the deep,
To break supinely on familiar shoals
Where one in childhood digged a mimic grave!

  .   .   .   .

Thank God for those few, momentary stars,
And that slow-lifting zone of topaz light,
Like parting guest returning with a smile.
We care not now that the insatiate storm
Plunges with leaps of thunder on the east.
                    (*The music ceases*)
Give me thy hand, dear one, though unto pain
I crush it to be sure that this be dream,
Knowing 'twas Death that passed, and oh, how near!

Let us examine the music for which these two poems were written. Chopin's *Fifteenth Prelude* is one of the most familiar of
piano works. It is based on two themes and is in regular ABA
form, the first section being in D flat major, and the second in C
sharp minor. Particularly noticeable is the continuous repetition
of the A flat, which changes enharmonically to G sharp and continues as a pedal-point in the middle section. It is possible that
Marston intended to suggest or imitate this effect by the (false)
river-forever rhyme which he keeps for the first and third lines of
each stanza throughout the poem. However, this cannot be assumed with any certainty, for the absence of anything corresponding to the marked contrast between the beginning and end of the

piece and the middle section (which is different both in key and in general style) would certainly show that he was not attempting to follow the music closely. There is an interesting conflict of testimony as to how far "hearers" really follow the music in their own minds after they have become interested in their interpretations. Weld found that visual imagery in his subjects was inclined to follow the structure of the music and to respond to changes of pitch and rhythm when these changes were important. However, Vernon Lee, on the strength of her questionnaires, writes:[12]

Indeed, I am convinced that what people describe as the "expression," the "message," or "meaning" of a piece of music, may answer merely to some prominent peculiarity which happens to be caught hold of, and committed *verbally* to memory, other effects being forgotten because they are not thus *verbally* identified and dwelt upon; as is the case with Pictrix [Lee's name for a woman who painted her impressions of music], who says that when she has begun to draw a "musical picture," she does not continue to attend to the music.

"Pictrix" explains that hence she draws, not a symphony or a movement, but a phrase, which may be modified in her mind, and in the details of her picture, by subsequent repetitions and developments. No doubt the act of drawing helps to take her mind away from the music, but, even making due allowance for that, it would seem that her case may be typical. In many poems on musical works the interpretations depart so radically from the form of the music that it is hardly conceivable that the authors actually followed the music after the germ of the idea of their interpretations had come to them. This lapse of musical attention, as well as the limitations of poetry previously discussed, would also help to explain why poets who attack a symphonic movement theme by theme and bar by bar through the initial section usually become vague and generalizing in the development section.

The second of these poems on Chopin follows the musical form, with a change of subject in the middle section. We see here many of the elements of musical description which have already been noted. There is, for example, a considerable use of synaesthesia. The vision suggested in the second poem has no possible connection with that in the first, except the presence of water (this, as well as another prelude of Chopin, is sometimes called the "Raindrop" Prelude), and this difference is typical. A third interpretation, differing widely from both of these, is given by a contemporary virtuoso who says, if I remember correctly, that to him this composition suggests a mother, who, while rocking her infant boy by the fire, falls asleep and dreams of seeing him grown to manhood and being led to the gallows; she then awakes and continues rocking the cradle.

In the *Histoire de ma vie,* George Sand gives an account[13] of the circumstances under which this prelude (or, according to some critics, the sixth) was composed:

There is one of them which occurred to him on a dismal rainy evening which produced a terrible mental depression. We had left him well that day, Maurice and I, and had gone to Palma to buy things we required for our encampment. The rain had come on, the torrents had overflowed, we had travelled three leagues in six hours to return in the midst of the inundation, and we arrived in the dead of night, without boots, abandoned by our driver, having passed through unheard-of dangers. We made haste, anticipating the anxiety of our invalid. It had been indeed great, but it had become as it were congealed into a kind of calm despair, and he played his wonderful prelude weeping. On seeing us enter he rose, uttering a great cry, then he said to us, with a wild look and in a strange tone: "Ah! I knew well that you were dead!"

When he had come to himself again, and saw the state in which we were, he was ill at the retrospective spectacle of our dangers; but he confessed to me afterwards that while waiting for our return he had seen all this in a dream and that, no longer distinguishing this dream from reality, he had grown calm and been almost lulled to sleep while playing the piano, believing that he was dead himself. He saw himself drowned in a lake; heavy and ice-cold drops of water fell at regular intervals upon his breast, and when I drew his attention to those drops of water which were actually falling at regular intervals upon the roof, he denied having heard them. He was even vexed at what I translated by the term imitative harmony. He protested with all his might, and he was right, against the puerility of these imitations for the ear. His genius was full of mysterious harmonies of nature, translated by sublime equivalents into his musical thought, and not by a servile repetition of external sounds. His composition of this evening was indeed full of the drops of rain which resounded on the sonorous tiles of the monastery, but they were transformed in his imagination and his music into tears falling from heaven on his heart.

It is well known that George Sand herself did not hesitate to improve a story, and her followers have made a number of variations on this one.[14] Hence it is impossible to know just what literary accounts or musical criticisms may have influenced Johnson's poem. It is reasonably certain that if he had been familiar with George Sand's own version of the story he would have followed it more closely, but almost every element of Johnson's poem is to be found in such criticisms as that of Kleczynski:[15]

The foundation of the picture is the drops of rain falling at regular intervals which by their continual patter bring the mind to a state of sadness; a melody full of tears is heard through the rush of the rain; then passing to the key of C sharp minor, it rises from the depths of the bass to a prodigious crescendo, indicative of the terror which nature in its deathly aspect excites in the heart of man. Here again the form does not allow the ideas to become too sombre; notwithstanding the melancholy which seizes you, a feeling of tranquil grandeur revives you.

Johnson uses the obvious ideas of George Sand and some of the criticisms inspired by her account. He has both tears and the falling of rain. The storm in progress during Chopin's dream, together with its natural corollary in human awe, is put into the middle section. Two flashes of lightning, the second nearer than the first, form the climax of the poem and represent the climax of the composition with its twice-played phrase:

Even the idea of being under water has been brought in, though it is introduced casually in a simile and may not be due either to Chopin's vision or to anything in the music. The woman is, of course, a reflection of George Sand. If we could safely assume that Johnson's poem is based on the music alone we would consider it a triumph of interpretation in that it reproduces a great many single details of the original vision — if we can trust George Sand. In the last analysis, however, it is impossible to say how much of the accuracy of Johnson's poem comes from coincidence, how much from biographical and critical sources, how much from vague, non-musical hints (such as the knowledge that George Sand and Chopin were in Majorca together), and how much from pure interpretation of the music. These very uncertainties help to make the poem a typical specimen of visual and narrative interpretation of music.

As an example of the power of suggestion of a title, we may take George Norton Northrop's poem on Grieg's *Einsamer Wanderer*:[16]

> Out on the bleak abandoned moor
> Begirt by shroud of storm-clouds drear
> And black treetrunks decayed and sere,
> The wanderer, clad in garments poor,
> Bends on his wearied way.
>
> Oft as he bows beneath the storm
> A mournful murmur breathes he low
> That mingles with the cutting snow
> And finds repose in icemailed form
> Of oak, the winds' shrill prey.

But soon his plodding footsteps cease;
The wanderer sinks beneath the blast;
The murky pall of night is cast;
The tempest shrieks; but he has peace
Among the stars alway.

The writer has here taken the idea expressed in the title, added to it the fact that Grieg was a nationalistic Norwegian composer, and drawn on his imagination for the rest. The shrill winds have no justification in the music; there is nothing which could be taken as imitative of the sound of wind, and the piece is on the whole very quiet, only twice rising to *forte*. As for the story, with its beginning, middle, and end, it simply cannot be fitted to the music, which falls into two halves, the second of which is an almost exact repetition of the first. Hence the wanderer should die twice or not at all! The only thing in the poem which seems to have any possible reference to Grieg's composition is the wanderer's "mournful murmur," which might easily refer to the bass at (a):

There are, however, several poems describing pieces of music largely by means of visual imagery which pay strict attention to the musical form and follow it closely. Frances Ridley Havergal's *The Moonlight Sonata* and Todhunter's *Dvorák's "Dumky" Trio*[17] are examples of this method, as are a number of the poems of Plattensteiner.

At this point we must consider what Vernon Lee calls "the imaginary composer." Many people make ideal heroes of the composers whom they particularly admire. Starting with some basis of biographical fact, they put all that they can read into the music into the life and character of the composer. Johnson's use of Majorca in his poem on the Chopin *Prelude*, as well as his allusions to George Sand, and Northrop's use of Norwegian climate

and scenery are mild examples of this tendency. Felicia Hemans'
verse on Mozart's *Requiem* is a better one. Beginning with the
facts that it was his last composition, was commissioned by a
stranger, and was performed at his funeral, she has worked up a
sentimental account of Mozart composing the *Requiem* with a
premonition that the stranger who had ordered it had come from
another world, and that Mozart was really composing it for his
own funeral. The last of the nine stanzas is typical:

> One more then, one more strain;
> To earthly joy and pain
> A rich, and deep, and passionate farewell!
> I pour each fervent thought,
> With fear, hope, trembling, fraught,
> Into the notes that o'er my dust shall swell.[18]

This habit of interpreting music in terms of the composer's life
is more prevalent than one might think. Even Wagner interpreted
Beethoven's *C Sharp Minor Quartette* as an account of the composer's thoughts and moods during the course of a day.[19] Beethoven, as the most loved and the most romanticized of composers,
has been the subject of more poetry of this type than any other
musician, and we shall see a good specimen (though well-docu-
mented rather than imagined) when we take up Masters' poem
in detail in Chapter VII. Two more examples will show the
lengths to which this type of poetry can go. Geibel's *Pergolesi*
(closely imitated from Tieck's), describes the first performance of
the *Stabat Mater,* with a number of inaccuracies which show conclusively that Geibel was not very familiar with the work, and at
the end, just before the "Fac me cruce custodiri," he has the Angels
interfere:

> Horsch! Da tönen Seraphslieder
> In den Chor der Frommen nieder,
> Wunder ahnend lauscht das Ohr;
> Endwärts steigen sel'ge Geister,
> Tragen himmelan den Meister,
> Und das Lied rauscht mit empor.[20]

Hark! the songs of the seraphim float down among the pious singers, and the
ear listens in expectation of a miracle. Finally the blessed spirits ascend, bear-
ing the master to heaven, and the song floats with them on high.

And merely on the strength of the name of *Weber's Last Waltz*
(which is really by Cramer), the Rev. W. Sewell found it to be a

"sweet and sadly solemn strain," "full of death and home" — a satisfied and peaceful, though somewhat melancholy, farewell to life![21]

Since a citation of any large proportion of the numerous interpretative visions would require an amount of space quite out of proportion to their importance, and since their most important characteristics have been illustrated by the extracts already given, we may now leave them with a brief summary of their main points.

The visions which are described as accompanying music may come from some conscious association in the hearer's mind, or they may be inexplicable. In genuine cases of hearers with strong visual imagery they are involuntary, but many writers, in an effort to reproduce the effect of music, formulate visions intentionally. Their theory seems to be that scenes and actions are more easily described than music, and, if carefully chosen, can create the same effects. Descriptive titles are always followed as far as their indications go; music from operas is connected with scenes from them, and the visual interpretations of vocal music in general follow suggestions in the words. Beyond this point, wide disagreements as to what any piece of music "represents" are the rule. Occasionally striking resemblances between different interpretations are found, but they must be accepted with caution, as we seldom know how far similar program-notes, remarks of biographers, or other external sources may have influenced two or more writers in the same direction. It seems to be impossible for a composer to convey any objective impressions to an audience, even by the most obvious imitations of natural sounds, and the poems recording musical visions prove that it is impossible for a poet to give his reader any conception of a piece of music by reporting the scenes which it called up in his own mind. Often, particularly in long poems, a series of visions will follow the music rather closely; just as often there will be no apparent connection between the verse and the composition, either in form or in spirit.

Many writers, particularly the more sentimental ones, tend to interpolate all their interpretations of a composer's music into his life and thoughts, sometimes in direct defiance of historical fact. Beethoven is the especial target of this type of interpretation, and we shall find it even more prevalent in the translation of music into moods than in the visual accounts studied in this chapter. The romanticized (and sentimentalized) Beethoven tradition is here seen in its full force, and it seems to continue unabated in spite of the attacks of a number of eminent critics. One critic even went so far as to reply, when someone urged that Beethoven's character must have contained all the wildness and gloom which this person found in his music: "You might as well say that because there's pepper in the soup, there's pepper in the cook!" The validity of this retort in its context may be open to question, but it is certainly a good answer to much of the interpretation of composers' lives on the basis of ideas and sentiments gathered from their works.

CHAPTER VI

Moods
and Moral
Allegory

Schopenhauer says that a Beethoven symphony gives us great apparent confusion, with perfect order underlying it all, and is thus a picture of the universe. He continues:[1]

Zugleich nun aber sprechen aus dieser Symphonie alle menschlichen Leidenschaften und Affekte: die Freude, die Trauer, die Liebe, der Hass, der Schrecken, die Hoffnung, usw. in zahllosen Nüancen, jedoch alle gleichsam nur in abstracto und ohne alle Besonderung: es ist ihre blosse Form, ohne den Stoff, wie eine blosse Geisterwelt, ohne Materie. Allerdings haben wir den Hang, sie, beim zuhören, zu realisieren, sie, in der Phantasie, mit Fleisch und Bein zu bekleiden und allerhand Szenen des Lebens und der Natur darin zu sehen. Jedoch befördert dies, im Ganzen genommen, nicht ihr Verständnis, noch ihren Genuss, gibt ihr vielmehr einen fremdartigen, willkürlichen Zusatz: daher ist es besser, sie in ihrer Unmittelbarkeit und rein anzufassen.

At the same time all human passions and affections — joy, sorrow, love, hate, terror, hope, etc. — speak from this symphony in innumerable nuances, but only in the abstract and without any specific application: it is their pure form, without material, like a spirit-world without matter. It is true that we have a tendency to *realize* them when we hear them, to clothe them with flesh and blood in our own fantasy and to see all sorts of scenes from life and nature in them. All things considered, however, this process requires neither an understanding nor an enjoyment of them, but rather gives an external, arbitrary addition. Therefore it is better to accept them purely and directly.

This theoretical statement showing at least one way in which visual interpretations are formed is supported by some of the answerers to Lee's questionnaires, one of whom says that music represents human emotions and that she sees it as a drama, but

96

the characters are always vague and disembodied — *he, she, it,* etc., without antecedents.[2] Perhaps the clearest account of this reaction to music is De Quincey's description[3] of its effects in his dreams:

Then suddenly would come a dream of far different character — a tumultuous dream — commencing with a music such as now I often heard in sleep — music of preparation and of awakening suspense. The modulations of fast-gathering tumults were like the opening of the Coronation Anthem; and, like *that,* gave a feeling of multitudinous movement, of infinite cavalcades filing off, and the tread of innumerable armies. The morning was come of a mighty day — a day of crisis and of ultimate hope for human nature, then suffering mysterious eclipse, and labouring in some dread extremity. Somewhere, but I knew not where — somehow, but I knew not how — by some beings, but I knew not by whom — a battle, a strife, an agony, was travelling through all its stages — was evolving itself, like the catastrophe of some mighty drama, with which my sympathy was the more insupportable from deepening confusion as to its local scene, its cause, its nature, and its undecipherable issue. . . . Then, like a chorus, the passion deepened. Some greater interest was at stake, some mightier cause, than ever yet the sword had pleaded, or trumpet had proclaimed. Then came sudden alarms; hurryings to and fro; trepidations of innumerable fugitives, I knew not whether from the good cause or the bad. . . .

Those who are more literal-minded, or at least less capable of dealing with abstractions, naturally tend to invent antecedents for the characters and issues vaguely delineated by the music and to give them pictorial interpretations. It is possible that those whose visual imagery is automatic really go through some such process without realizing it. We shall see later that interpretation by moral allegory is a process similar to this, except that, instead of giving these vague emotions human characters and antecedents, the hearer, while retaining their abstract form, gives them cosmic significance.

Many writers, however, are content to leave them as vague, disembodied emotions, and to treat of them in this form. Weld finds that the emotional experiences of musical auditors are really moods rather than emotions in the ordinary sense of the term, and concludes[4] that, with some exceptions,

We may safely say that music of a certain sort may easily arouse such a mood as may be expressed in terms of confidence, yearning, imploring tenderness, mysteriousness, lightness or daintyness, elevation, joy, triumph, etc., but in every case the listener must give himself up to the music and allow it to become the expression of his own feeling.

E. T. A. Hoffmann often interprets music thus in terms of moods.

and we find many examples in poems on musical compositions. John Payne's poem on Field's *Nocturne in D Minor*[5] uses this method exclusively: the composition is interpreted as an expression of autumnal melancholy, and the only possible reference to the music is the misleading one to a non-existent cuckoo-motif. More often, we find lists of emotions or moods aroused by a piece of music. Todhunter writes of Chopin's *Nocturnes* that

> There the wild dæmons that in us rave and sigh —
> Pride, Love, Grief, Joy, Despair, and Melancholy,
> Robed for their parts in Life's high tragedy,
> Like stately knights and damsels moving slowly
> To music, pass in sumptuous pageant by.[6]

And F. A. Kemble, writing *On a Symphony of Beethoven*,[7] finds Schopenhauer's entire universe present in it, with particular emphasis on a Schopenhauer-like view of life:

> Terrible music, whose strange utterance
> Seemed like the spell of some dread conscious trance;
> Motionless misery, impotent despair,
> With beckoning visions of things dear and fair;
> Restless desire, sharp poignant agonies;
> Soft, thrilling, melting, tender memories;
> Struggle and tempest, and, around it all,
> The heavy muffling folds of some dark pall
> Stifling it slowly; a wild wail for life
> Sinking in darkness — a short, passionate strife
> With hideous fate, crushing the soul to earth;
> Sweet snatches of some melancholy mirth;
> A creeping fear, a shuddering dismay,
> Like the cold dawning of some fatal day;
> Dim faces growing pale in distant lands;
> Departing feet, and slowly severing hands;
> Voices of love speaking the words of hate, —
> The mockery of a blessing come too late;
> Loveless and hopeless life, with memory, —
> This curse that music seemed to speak to me.

The reference to fate and a number of other fragments of evidence make it very probable that the symphony here described is the *Fifth*. C. P. Cranch has a sonnet[8] on the same work which also interprets it largely in terms of moods, though with considerably more moral allegory than is found in this poem. Gilder's poem[9] on Tschaikowsky's *Symphonie Pathétique* is another example chosen from among the many expressions of music in moods, and this time the mood is a morbid, despairing one:

> When the last movement fell, I thought: Ah me!
> Death this indeed; but still the music poured
> On and still on. Oh, deathlier it grew
> And then, at last, my beating heart stood still, —
> Beyond all natural grief that music passing,
> Beyond all tragedy or last farewell.
> Then, on that fatal tide, dismayed I felt
> This living soul, my own, without one tear,
> Slowly, irrevocably, and alone,
> Enter the ultimate silence and the dark.

Here both verbal suggestion and biographical fact (Tschaikowsky's death soon after the completion of this symphony gave it a sentimental appeal which caused it to be tremendously popular for a number of years) play their part in suggesting Gilder's reaction to the symphony. Rosa Newmarch's sonnet[10] on this same composition interprets it universally as a representation of the struggle between man and destiny (one of the favorite moral allegories), and in her biography of the composer she discusses this interpretation and gives her reasons for choosing it rather than the common personal one which sees in the symphony Tschaikowsky's premonition of his own approaching death.[11]

Gilder felt his own soul go through the despair which he attributed to Tschaikowsky's, and most writers who deal with music as a representation of emotions state that it creates these emotions in the hearer. There is, however, a different type which considers the music as presenting an idea to the intellect rather than setting a mood for the emotions, and a distinction between these two types definitely exists, although it is so fine that often it cannot be exactly drawn. In one type the music will arouse in the hearer the emotion which he understands it to represent; in the other, it will suggest this emotion in the abstract. Henri Allorge sees Wagner's *Tristan* as an expression of physical desire:[12]

> C'est un mélange altier de sanglants héroïsmes,
> D'angoisse, de folie et de ravissements;
> C'est la fureur d'aimer et tous ses paroxysmes,
> La passion farouche et ses égarements.
>
> C'est le désir vainqueur qui dessèche les lèvres,
> Et qui fait tressaillir l'ivresse des baisers
> Au fond des membres las, où bouillonnent des fièvres,
> Et dans les yeux aigus, où flambent des brasiers.
>
> La frénésie insatiable des étreintes
> Gronde; un feu rugissant dans les veines se tord;

Le cri d'espoir se mêle aux suppliantes plaintes,
Et le chant triomphal s'unit au chant de mort.

It is a lofty mixture of bloody, heroic deeds, anguish, madness, and rapture; it is the violence of love and all its paroxysms, fierce passion and its excesses.

It is the conquering desire which dries the lips and which makes the intoxication of kisses tremble in weary limbs seething with fevers, and in piercing eyes where live coals blaze.

The insatiable frenzy of embraces cries out; a roaring fire twists through the veins; the cry of hope mixes with supplicating lamentations, and the song of triumph becomes one with the song of death.

Allorge goes on to say that the music may make lovers long for a happy death together, but there is no hint that the crisis of sexual desire which he takes the music to represent is reproduced in the audience. Nor does he consider that the music has failed, as Gilder would have felt had the *Pathétique* failed to depress him. Allorge simply considers that the music portrays these emotions, without forcing them on the listener.

In emotional responses to music we find two distinct types which Lee classifies as "Apollonian" and "Dionysiac," taking the terms from Nietzsche:

Apollo steht vor mir als der verklärende Genius des principii individuationis, durch den allein die Erlösung in Scheine wahrhaft zu erlangen ist: während unter dem mystischen Jubelruf des Dionysos der Bann der Individuation zersprengt wird und der Weg zu den Müttern des Seins, zu dem innersten Kern der Dinge offen liegt.[13]

Apollo appears to me as the transfiguring genius of the *principium individuationis,* and through him alone apparent release is truly attainable; whereas with the mystical shout of rejoicing of Dionysos the bond of individual being is shattered and a path is laid open to the Mothers of Being, to the innermost heart of things.

Lee applies these terms to the calm and the excitable types of auditors respectively. The Apollonian type hears music with a feeling of infinite peace and repose; to him it is a solution of all difficulties, a final synthesis of life, perfect, complete, and satisfying. The Dionysiac auditor is excited by music as a savage by the insistent beat of drums (or a cultivated audience by Ravel's *Bolero*); it arouses in him a feeling of energy that must be expended, and leaves him, not satisfied, as the Apollonian is, but excited and restless. The fundamental difference between these two types of auditors may best be explained by a poem exemplifying each. For the

Apollonian point of view we shall take Edna Millay's *On Hearing a Symphony of Beethoven*:[14]

> Sweet sounds, oh, beautiful music, do not cease!
> Reject me not into the world again.
> With you alone is excellence and peace,
> Mankind made plausible, his purpose plain.
> Enchanted in your air benign and shrewd,
> With limbs a-sprawl and empty faces pale,
> The spiteful and the stingy and the rude
> Sleep like the scullions in the fairy-tale.
> This moment is the best the world can give:
> The tranquil blossom on the tortured stem.
> Reject me not, sweet sounds! Oh, let me live
> Till Doom espy my towers and scatter them,
> A city spell-bound under the aging sun,
> Music my rampart, and my only one.

An unnamed poem[15] of Ricarda Huch, expressing the Dionysiac reaction to music, stands in sharp contrast to the preceding verse:

> Ausgegossen, Musik,
> Über die feilschende Welt,
> Allerschütternde, lösest du
> Unserer trägen Geschäftigkeit
> Sklavenjoch endlich.
> Hochatmend in dir,
> Krieg'risches Element,
> Mitten durch Schwerter trägst du uns,
> Sterbend Unsterbliche,
> Lorbeertrunken und frei.

Poured out over the haggling world, all-shaking music, you finally release us from the slavish yoke of our lazy activity. Breathing deeply the warrior element, you carry us, dying immortals, through the midst of swords, drunk with glory and free.

The difference between these two verses is as great as that between the Oriental search for Nirvana and Nietzsche's ecstatic striving towards the superman. Both attitudes are common enough. Further examples of the Apollonian attitude are to be found in Alfred Neumann's *J. S. Bach: Suite Nr. 3 in C-Dur, Sarabande,*[16] and Catherine Parmenter's *On Hearing Schubert's "Unfinished Symphony,"*[17] while Amy Lowell's *After Hearing a Waltz by Bartók*[18] is another good specimen of the pure Dionysiac reaction.

As a rule, these attitudes are not quite so sharply defined as they would appear to be from these examples. In the description of specific compositions, especially, it is often difficult to judge how much is response to the particular music in question and how much is characteristic of the poet's attitude towards music in general. However, the distinction between these two types of hearers may help to explain differences such as that between the two poems on Beethoven's *Fifth Symphony* mentioned above, where one writer found it a collection of woes, with merely enough joy to be mocking, and defined it as a curse, while the other found it a final victory over adverse powers, resulting in a conclusion of peace and hope.

Sometimes emotional and even visual responses to music are influenced by arbitrary factors which might easily pass unnoticed. One of these elements is what Carl Spitteler calls "orchestral allegory"[19] — the habit, coming largely from literary references, of giving an arbitrary significance to certain instruments. He discusses the effects of this predetermined association on musical composition, and shows that, in opera especially, where some mood or circumstance must be clearly predominant at a given time, composers are inclined to choose their orchestration by the names and associative values of the instruments, regardless of their actual sound and their place in the musical fabric. He points out a number of cases where a blind following of some preconceived idea as to what an instrument should express has led to definitely bad orchestration. The effect on the interpreters of music is far more obvious than this influence on composers. We repeatedly find instruments interpreted according to Spitteler's groupings. Thus Allorge, in his poem[20] on the horn, gives it a decidedly romantic function, and the anonymous author of *Das Orchester* comments on the usual interpretation of anything connected with the horn:

> Es ist ein heikles Beginnin,
> Wenn einer aufs Horn sich verlegt,
> Wenn nicht romantisches Sinnen
> Und Träumen die Seele bewegt.[21]

It's a ticklish undertaking to talk about the horn without getting one's soul involved in romantic notions and dreams.

Romantic poetry is full of the horn (preferably heard at some distance, in a forest, from a tower, by moonlight), and these associations are likely to appear wherever there is an extended reference to the horn. Similarly, the oboe almost invariably calls forth pastoral pictures and ideas. To a lesser extent, all the instruments mentioned by Spitteler in his list have a strong tendency to be interpreted according to his classification. He attempts to explain how the significance of each of these groups, and of each instrument, arose, and we thus see that interpretation by instrumental allegory is merely another form of interpretation by association of ideas. However, it has the advantage that, since the association is generally standardized, poetic uses of it will be readily understood by most readers.

In passing, we may mention an extreme case of another type of instrumental allegory. Eugène Manuel has a sonnet[22] on the serpent the point of which lies in the irony of the serpent's being found in a church orchestra, where it is forced to praise God. Although the symbolism here comes originally from the shape of the serpent, which gave it its name, it is probable that it was the name which gave Manuel the idea of his sonnet, and thus the poem is another case of association of words. Naturally, the sonnet has no musical meaning whatsoever, as the author has no concern for the alleged musical qualities of the instrument: he is concerned only with its name and shape and with the symbolical use that can be made of them.

Many auditors are satisfied with the disembodied emotions of which Schopenhauer speaks, but others, by trying to create situations to explain them, arrive at interpretations in terms of incidents or stories. Still a third class is puzzled by emotions that it cannot understand. Auditors of this type feel emotions when they hear music, but they do not presume to be able to tell what originally caused them, and this inability completely to understand the composer gives them a feeling of frustration in listening to music. Probably the clearest statement of this point of view — though an exaggerated and somewhat morbid one — is that given by the half-insane narrator in Tolstoi's *Kreutzer Sonata*.[23] A military march, he says, produces a desire to walk in step; the soldiers actually do march in time to it, and its goal is achieved. A similar statement can be made about some other types, such as dance-music. But a work like the *Kreutzer Sonata* (or any other piece of absolute music) carries the auditor through a cycle of meaningless feelings. Beethoven knew what caused these feelings in him, and his composition, like the marching of the soldiers, carried them through to their proper goal. To his audience, however, they are simply excitement which has no basis in experience and which leads to no action. Hence they leave one with a feeling of irritation and emotional frustration. Music, therefore, is morally evil.

To hearers less neurotic than Tolstoi's narrator a symphony becomes a sibylline utterance, something fraught with a high significance, but a significance which forever eludes the listener, who can infer and guess to his heart's content, but can never know. And these persons are not satisfied with inferences and guesses. We must distinguish sharply between those who interpret a particular piece of music as an *expression* of mystery and those who feel that music in general is an expression of various moods, but *is* an eternal mystery to the listener because he is incapable of knowing why these moods ever arose or what significance he should attach to them.

John Todhunter frequently questions music as to its meaning, but when he asks:

> Tell me why, skipping suddenly in,
> With change abrupt, that freaksome strain,
> With its mirth remote and thin
> Has now possest the violin?[24]

or,

> Is it a dirge some poor soul sings,
> Left by a grave alone
> While in a funeral march, with muted strings
> Viol and violin moan?[25]

we feel that he is merely using the device of the rhetorical question to state his own interpretation of the music — an interpretation of which he is singularly positive.

Many writers, however, are genuinely mystified by music, since it seems to say something definite to them, and something important, but something which they are powerless to express in concrete terms. The most complete presentation of this hopeless questioning of music is to be found in the sestet of Henry Aylett Sampson's sonnet, *The Death of Ase*:[26]

> For whom these tears that all unbidden rise?
> What star, now dust, looked on an agony
> That had no hearer as its grief outpoured?
> No answer in the moaning music lies,
> And at the shadowy Gate of Mystery
> Stands the mute angel with the lifted sword.

Vernon Lee several times takes up the question of the "message" of music, and she finds that practically all but the intellec-

tual and analytical listeners are firmly convinced that there is
some message in any good composition, and that this message is
something which should be expressible in words. It is true that
a few hearers are content to say that music gives them some great
ideas or truths without saying, or attempting to say, what these are.
Thus Lissauer speaks of the *Adagio* of Bruckner's *String Quin-
tette:*

> Urblatt du, raunend Stille,
> Schrift der Musiksibylle,
> Verlautbart durch einen dumpfen Mund
> Aller Erde — und Himmelweisheit kund.[27]

Primeval page, whispering silence, writing of the Sibyl of music, all the
wisdom of heaven and earth revealed through a muffled mouth.

Such affirmation of a great message, without any attempt at a
verbal rendition of it, is rare, and would seem to require a particularly good musical sense.*
    Fuller-Maitland, for example, felt at times the conviction that
music held some message, but he was a musician and hence
realized that even if music had some valuable message any attempt
at a verbal rendition of it was doomed to failure. He writes:[28]

There are places in the orchestral works of Brahms where I feel as if words
were on the point of being uttered; just as when one tries at the moment of
waking to lay hold on the garment of an escaping dream, so in the *andante
sostenuto* of the First Symphony the oboe passage in bars 7 to 13 never fails
to give me the impression that some verbal message of utter beauty and significance will bless the world if only I can catch and hold it.

Vernon Lee gives here and there a number of explanations of this
conviction of the existence of some verbal message in music, but
they need not detain us here, since none of them throws any light
on the processes by which poets seek to capture these meanings and
express them in poetic form. It should be noticed that a number
of poets have, even while attempting to extract the "message" from
music, admitted that it is largely subjective and will vary with
different auditors, or even with the same auditor on different occa-

---

*In this connection the entire last chapter, "Poetry and Beliefs," of I. A. Richards'
Principles of Literary Criticism is extraordinarily interesting. It shows that a poem
(or any other work of art) may produce a feeling of belief without the reader's
having any idea just *what* is believed. Frequently the reader attaches the belief to
some "illegitimate object," such as the idea of immortality at the conclusion of
Adonais. Doubtless the whole question of the "message" of music is one of finding
something to which to attach this feeling in an art which makes no explicit statements.

sions. We have already seen Gilder's statement that music is "ever the same, with message never the same," and Conrad Aiken elaborates the differing interpretations given by different auditors of a restaurant orchestra. After giving one version he comments:[29]

> So says the tune to you — but what to me?
> What to the waiter as he pours your coffee?
> The violinist as he suavely draws his bow?
> That man, who folds his paper, overhears it,
> A thousand dreams revolve and fall and flow.

He then proceeds to give another interpretation entirely different from the first.

Hearers who are troubled by the varying scenes or recollections which music can evoke, or who feel dissatisfied when emotions are produced in them without their being able to say what originally caused them, or who feel that a great composition must carry some message of vast and eternal significance, very frequently resort to the interpretation of music by moral allegory. Schopenhauer says that music flatters the will-to-live by imitating its nature and predicting its triumph and final peace.[30] This prediction of a happy human destiny is one of the favorite themes of the moral allegorists, though it must be admitted that the interpretation as death or fate triumphant over life or hope is equally common. These two standard interpretations, taken together, form the theme of about three-fourths of the poems of moral allegory.

The reason for the existence of this method of dealing with music is clear. A listener feels something which to him seems to be an emotion of joy, but he cannot say what has produced this joy. Furthermore, he senses some vital message in the composition. Thus a casual scene, even in the composer's life, which might satisfy some of the describers who use pictures or stories will not suffice for his conception of the music. What, then, is more natural than that he should personify an abstraction under the form of this theme, which then ceases to be a joyous theme or an expression of any picture or transient idea, and becomes Joy (the capital is characteristic) itself? Similarly, a cheerful theme becomes Hope, and a strident one, crashing through the rest of the orchestra, is very likely to become Fate. (Tschaikowsky gave this meaning to the rhythmic theme which opens his *Fourth Symphony*, disappears for a while, and then returns to a dominating position in the last movement. Beethoven's remark about the opening theme of his *Fifth Symphony* — "So pocht das Schicksal an die Pforte"[31] — is another case in point.)

Here, again, words tend to come between the poet and the music, probably because poets are so accustomed to thinking in words that most of them find it difficult to follow pure musical thought, or even to believe in its existence. The way in which the ideas of moral allegory are born is well described by an answerer to one of Lee's questionnaires:[32]

Music for me expresses mystical emotion, the joy or sorrow of great Powers unembodied in any actual form. One has no exact impression, but vague phrases such as 'the whole Earth groaning and travailing together' — 'the joys and sorrows of humanity,' or of natural Powers, e. g. the wind, or of vague Teutonic Deities, express the 'ideas' I get from music. I hear the cry of the Outcasts (who they may be I haven't a clear notion), of souls unborn or 'lost,' of the 'spirits wandering about in desolate places seeking rest and finding none,' and so forth.

The writer of this passage was a man of letters, and he gives us a good conception of the way in which interpretations of music in terms of moral allegory arise. The phrases which he says music suggests to him, the vague powers — everything, even to the extensive use of capitals, is familiar to anyone who has studied many poems on music. It is interesting to note further that one of his phrases on music is already an iambic pentameter.

Once the allegorical personifications of musical themes are accepted, they follow the form of the composition with varying degrees of closeness. Were these figures static, they would merely be another example of the understanding of music as an expression of general ideas, but they move through a drama, and, almost invariably, through a conflict with each other. This method of interpretation is applied to the larger musical forms more extensively than to short compositions, for the obvious reason that a symphony naturally seems more significant than a prelude or an impromptu, and, more important still, its form is particularly adapted to the making of moral allegories. Any movement in sonata form, for example, will have its two principal contrasting themes which, in their statement and development, offer a ready-made allegory to the poet. He has only to name one of them. It then follows that the other is its contrary: if the first subject be Hope, the second will doubtless be Fate, and if the first be Despair, the second will usually be Triumph. The first movement of the symphony will set the stage and give the first battle of the two great powers; the second and third movements will present moods of one or the other of them (thus, if a first movement represents Fate and Hope, an *andante* may be resignation and a *scherzo* joyous abandon); and the finale will give the ultimate victory to one of the original powers. Cranch's *Beethoven's Fifth Symphony* is a fair example of the short poem of this type:[33]

> The mind's deep history here in tones is wrought,
> The faith, the struggle of the aspiring soul,
> The confidence of youth, the chill control
> Of manhood's doubts by stern experience taught;
> Alternate moods of bold and timorous thought,
> Sunshine and shadow — cloud and aureole;
> The failing foothold as the shining goal
> Appears, and truth so long, so fondly sought
> Is blurred and dimmed. Again and yet again
> The exulting march resounds. We must win now!
> Slowly the doubts resolve in clearer air.
> Bolder and grander the triumphal strain
> Ascends. Heaven's light is glancing on the brow,
> And turns to boundless hope the old despair.

Both lack of space and the prescribed poetical form of the sonnet prevent its following the structure of a symphony, but in the next chapter we shall make a study of a longer poem interpreting a sonata as a moral allegory. Interpretation of this type usually follows the musical structure with the same limitations that we have observed elsewhere: the opening themes can be followed bar by bar, but the complications, combinations, and metamorphoses of themes in the development section are beyond the powers of the poet's medium, and for these parts we usually find a passage simply saying that the two principles are at war. Except for this limitation, interpretation by moral allegory is usually well correlated with the music, and it is almost always possible to tell, in the more detailed examples, what point in the music the poet has reached. This was not true of the poems on music as a representation of scenes or pictures, but the allegorist draws his subject matter from the fundamental basis of musical form, whereas the other interpreters usually depend on adventitious associations and suggestions; hence the greater accuracy of the allegorical poems.

Since writers of these verses seem to have more interest in the music as such, their works almost always combine interpretation with actual description. In this, also, they offer a direct contrast to the users of visual imagery, who frequently write a long poem on a symphony without a single reference to the music. Even in the sonnet just quoted there was an allusion to "the exulting march," and the longer works in this type frequently keep interpretation and description parallel throughout. Thus any reader familiar with the composition in question can fully understand the poet's treatment of it, and even if the reader does not know the work he at least gets some vague impression of its general nature.

If music is to be interpreted as meaning anything beyond itself — anything capable of being expressed in words — there is no doubt that moral allegory is by far the best type of interpretation. It avoids the dilemma of synaesthesia, which is practically certain either to be meaningless or to contradict the reader's own impression. It escapes the definiteness of visual interpretation, and is thus much more readily acceptable to persons who do not see visions when hearing music, as well as more credible to those who themselves make similar interpretations, for the vagueness of the personified "Powers" makes them less likely to conflict with other conceptions than is a definite interpretation in terms of landscape or a dance. It avoids the static uninterestingness of simply identifying emotions and occasionally having one give way to another without apparent plan or reason. Finally, it succeeds moderately well in discarding accidental associations and suggestions, and thus, in its imitations of musical form, gets to the essential principles of music. Even if we do not grant that allegorical interpretations of this type reach any meaning consciously formulated by the composer, the fact remains that any artist's philosophy of life is more or less visible in his works, and it is certain that those poets who seek abstract ideas in them are far nearer to the truth than those who find biographical details or representations of the external world.

CHAPTER VII

The Elements Combined

So far we have tried, though not always successfully, to choose our examples so as to isolate the points under discussion and thus simplify their analysis. It must now be admitted, however, that this method is somewhat artificial. Though each poet who has written much on musical subjects specializes in some particular type of treatment, none confines himself exclusively to any type. All the authorities who have classified the different reactions to music have been careful to make the same general reservation. In any author who has written much about music we can find some examples of every approach which we have studied, and it is hard to find even a single poem of more than a few lines which consistently follows any single method throughout.

Hence it is desirable, now that we know the various elements which enter into the poetic treatment of musical compositions, to choose some of the longer and more interesting poems on familiar pieces of music and examine them in some detail, in order to see how these elements which we have discussed separately are combined in actual practice.

For this purpose we shall select Plattensteiner's poem on Beethoven's *IX. Symphonie*,[1] Todhunter's *Beethoven's "Sonata Appassionata,"*[2] and Edgar Lee Masters' *Beethoven's Ninth Symphony and the King Cobra*.[3] Since Beethoven has been far more extensively treated by poets than any other composer, poems dealing with his compositions offer the best examples, and the use of two widely different treatments of the same composition will show

110

something of the variety of treatment of musical works which has
been observed in the course of this study.

We shall begin with Plattensteiner's poem:

I.

Fernher Beben —, durch die Erde zittert
Dumpfes Rollen. — Donnernd läuft es bis ans End' der Welt. —
Aufgrellt Blitz —, krachend bricht die Welt zusammen,
Deine Welt! Sie ist gewesen? — Doch du bäumst dich auf,
5 Dein harmlos Freudigsein tat keinem weh.
Schriller fuhr ein zweiter Blitz zur Erde,
Heil'gen Traum von Heim und Herd verbrennend. —
Ach, dein Glück! Du sahst im Traum ein Paradies. —
Aus dem wüsten Trümmerhaufen sprühen Funken
10 Letzter Freude, die du bargst im Herzen! —
Wie ein nächt'ger Spuk zieht's noch einmal vorbei,
Das Ersehnte, das Geliebte dieser Erde. —
Wachsend bohren sich die Arme in den leeren Raum. —
Weltenwende! — Kniend hörst du rings die Welt zertrümmern.—
15 Birg im Herzen noch dein Restchen Schimmer
Von dem einst'gen Glück und rufe
In die Einsamkeit dein Lied! — Du hörst doch keinen Widerhall.

II

Nun denn, es sei!
Und geht es nicht zu ändern,
20 So schwing dich, Seele, über dieses Los
Und rufe der kleinen Freuden
Unabsehbar färb'ge Kette!
Kommt! Drängt immerzu heran!
Ist's möglich? Immer dichter wird die Kette!
25 Sieh, da wimmelt ihr Gedränge!
Wie dich neckend, dringen Wellen
Näher, und — sie haben dich erreicht. —
Gebt ihr mir Ersatz für andres?
Ja und ja, reicht mir die Hände,
30 Bin so froh, dass ihr gekommen.
Schwingt die Bänder, weist die Farben,
Dass ich lach' in euer Blau!
Ich versteh': die Menge muss es machen.
Farb'ges Band, du, ohne Ende
35 Durch die Erde unaufhaltsam ziehst du dich,
Wachsen willst du in den Himmel! — Blitz und Donner! —
Unaufhaltsam graue Wogen
Jagen alle Freuden fort,
Sie verschlingend? — Und doch nicht!
40 Farb'ge Punkte dort durchbrechen
Die zerriss'ne graue Wand.

Hin und Her noch wogt das Ringen —.
Wieder zieht der holde Reigen
Ohne Ende, dich erreichend.—
45 Mag es donnern, mag es blitzen,
Schlusspunkt ist noch nicht gemacht.
Langsam schwingst du dich doch höher,
Blitz und Donner unter dir. —

III

In Verklärung geistert Stille
50 In dem Wald und in der Flur.
Deine Seele dehnt sich wieder,
Frieden sehnend, weit im Raum.
Alles Leid verändert wehe
Züge merklich, da die guten Geister
55 Dir mit geberfrohen Händen nahen.
Schützend fluten dichte, grüne
Wände nieder, bergen dich dem Aug' der Welt. —
Lange war dir nicht so wohl,
Und du fühlst dich wie befreit.
60 Balsam schliesst die tausend Wunden,
Im Behagen tiefer Freude
Sprudeln alle Quellen wieder,
Und du träumst erneut den heil'gen Traum. —
Dürfen schmerzdurchfurchte Lippen ihn noch nennen?
65 Traum in dir, ach künde ihn,
Bist du wieder ausser dir!
Kannst dein bitt'res Schicksal du vergessen?
Ruft es streng, wie mahnend, aus der Höhe.
Sinke, Mahnung, in den Freiden
70 Meiner stummen Seele ein!
Bald wird hell ein Lied ertönen
Von dem dunklen Hintergrund der Leiden,
Das erblühen wird und muss dem Licht. —

IV

Polternd brechen ganze Wände ein. —
75 Doch, — es irrt mich nimmer.
So zerbrich! Du Schwacher, in die Knie!
Lasse ich mich nimmer täuschen,
Alle Prüfung ist zu Ende. —
Helft mir noch, ihr kleinen Freuden,
80 Jetzt weist Farben, werft die Bänder!
Dass ich einsam, auf dem Felsen stehend,
Künden kann mein hohes Lied,
Les' es ab von euren färb'gen Noten. —
Früher darf ich nicht verstummen,
85 Bis ich diese Antwort sang. —

Ihr vernahmt es, gute Geister,
Stimmt ihr es doch leise an!
Bebend zieht's durch meine Seele,
Allgewaltig drängend, schwellend,
90 Unsichtbar singt's mit der Chor. —
Doch ihr andern wisst noch nicht,
Was es kündet, ehe es nicht Worte taten. —
Da, Bewegung! — Dräuen möchte neue Prüfung? —
Jetzt die Antwort! Schwing dich auf in Klarheit, Lied!
95 Höchste Freude bringe und verbinde
Ungezählter leidgeprüfter Freunde Seelen
Zu dem heil'gen Bruderbund!
Dass sie alle es mit mir erkennen:
Über allem Einzelschicksal
100 Thront ein hoher Ordnungswille,
Der die weite Welt bis dicht zum Rande
Weisheitsvoll mit Art und Richtung füllt.
Trinkt ihr alle, durst'ge Seelen,
Nun erlöste durch mein Lied!

I

Distant trembling — a muffled rumbling quakes through the earth. — It rushes thundering to the ends of the world. — Lightning shrills — the world collapses with a crash, your world! — But you rear up; your innocent happiness harmed no one. A shriller second flash descends on the earth, consuming sacred dreams of hearth and home. — Alas for your happiness! You saw a paradise in a dream. From the desolate ruins spurt the last sparks of joy which you hid in your heart! — The longed-for, the beloved things of this earth pass before you again, like a ghost in the night. — The growing arms push out into empty space. Turning-point of the universe! Kneeling, you hear the world fall in ruins about you. Hide the little remnant of your former joy in your heart and cry your song out into the loneliness. — But you will hear no echo.

II

Well then, so be it. And if is beyond your power to change things, soul, rise above this fate and call the illimitable colored chain of little joys! Come! Keep crowding in! Is it possible? The chain grows more and more compact. See, crowds of them swarm here. As if to tease you, waves of them crowd closer, and — they have reached you. — Will you give me a substitute for other things? Yes, indeed; give me your hands. I am so glad that you have come. Swing your ribbons; show the colors, so that I may rejoice in your azure hue. I understand: the crowd must do it. Colored chain, you endlessly, unceasingly move about the earth, and wish to grow into the heavens! — Thunder and lightning! — Irresistible gray clouds drive all joys away; swallowing them up? — But no! There are points of color breaking through the torn gray wall. The struggle still sways back and forth. — Once again the lovely

endless row of dancers comes to you. Whether it thunder or lighten, the end
has not yet come. Slowly you soar higher, the thunder and lightning beneath
you. —

III

Transfigured quiet broods over the forest and meadow. Your soul, longing
for peace, again stretches out into space. All suffering markedly changes sad
features, when the good spirits approach you with generous hands. Thick
green walls flow down protectingly and hide you from the world's eye. — It
is long since you have felt so contented, and you have a sense of release.
Balsam heals your thousand wounds; in the enjoyment of deep peace all
springs gush again, and again you dream your sacred dream. — Can lips
scarred by pain be allowed to name it? The dream in you — oh, proclaim it
in your ecstasy! Can you forget your bitter fate? Cry it out, loud and warning,
from the heights. Sink into the peace of my silent soul, O exhortation! Soon,
from the dark background of sorrow, a song will ring out clearly, a song
that is to blossom and must reach the light.

IV

The walls give way with a crash. — But — I am not wrong. Shatter, then!
Fall to your knees, weakling! I cannot be deceived: all trials are ended. —
Help me still, you little joys: show your colors now; throw your streamers!
So that I, standing alone on the rock, can announce my lofty song — can
read it off from your colored notes. — I could not be silent until I sang this
answer. You understand it, good spirits; strike it up softly. Trembling, it
pierces my soul, omnipotently thrusting, swelling out. The chorus invisibly
joins in. But the rest of you do not understand its message until words explain
it. — There, movement! — Do new trials threaten? Now the answer! Swing
up, song, into the pure light. Bring the highest joy, and bind the souls of
innumerable friends, tested by suffering, in the holy bond of brotherhood!
Let them all realize, with me, that above the fate of any individual is throned
a high, ordering power which wisely fills the world to its rim with method
and direction. Drink, O thirsty souls now redeemed by my song.

Before beginning the discussion of this poem, we may remark
that it is fairly typical of Plattensteiner, though it probably contains more identifiable references to the music than most of his
poems. Some of them, in fact, have nothing which can be identified as specifically connected with any part of the music, and but
for their titles we should never suspect that they were related to
another art.

A casual reading of this poem shows that Plattensteiner has attempted to fit the entire symphony together into one definite and
unified philosophical program, developing from movement to
movement. All program interpreters of this symphony have made
similar attempts,[4] and there is the justification that, if a symphony

is an organic musical whole, any interpretation of it should present
a unity of thought. However, it is interesting to see what a musician has to say on the subject:[5]

It must be here said that no connection need be looked for between the
first three movements of the Choral Symphony and the 'Ode to Joy' which
inspired its *Finale.* The very title of the work — Beethoven's own — is con-
clusive on this point. It is not a Symphony on Schiller's Ode to Joy, but it
is a Symphony with Final Chorus on Schiller's Ode to Joy — 'Sinfonie mit
Schluss-Chor über Schillers Ode an die Freude.' Beethoven, says an intelligent critic,[6] 'has not given us any programme to the first movement, nor even
a descriptive title, as he does in the Pastoral Symphony.' The first three
movements might have had another *Finale* — indeed, they nearly had one
[...]; and it is not necessary to attempt to reconcile either the opening
Allegro, the *Scherzo* (so called), or the *Adagio* with the train of thought and
feeling suggested by the Ode which is embodied in the latter portion of the
work. In fact, as we shall see farther on, Beethoven tries the three first movements one after the other, to see if any of them will suit for a *Finale, and
rejects them all!*

Plattensteiner's first phrase, "Fernher Beben, — durch die Erde
zittert dumpfes Rollen," refers to the opening bars of the symphony, in which the tonic and dominant of an A chord are sustained by the second violins and 'cellos, tremolo, along with the
horns, while the other strings come down, by leaps on the same
notes, from the E at the top of the treble stave to the A at the
bottom of the bass, repeating this phrase twice, and each time
hurrying it. The omission of the mediant of the chord keeps the
tonality indefinite. This vague introduction gives way to a *fortissimo* passage for the entire orchestra, easily identified as Plattensteiner's "Blitz":

A short passage, represented by the next two lines of the poem,
follows this, and then the second flash of lightning symbolizes the
same figure as before, given this time in the key of B flat. It should
be noticed that the repetition of the introductory part (the "Beben") is not mentioned, and from this point onward we find it
difficult to follow the course of the music with any certainty. The
joys that remain, and the last spectral procession of the longed-for

and loved things of the world may well refer to the melody beginning at bar 74:

At this point any detailed following of the music ceases, and the
extended and remarkable development of the "lightning" subject,
with all its wealth of subsidiary motives, is summed up in the
phrase: "Wachsend bohren sich die Arme in den leeren Raum,"
and the following statement of the destruction of the world. At
the conclusion of the movement we have what is probably another
specific allusion to the music, in lines 15-18. Several critics, including Grove, have mentioned the "affecting wail" of the oboes (bar
514, ff.) as an expression of loneliness and grief:

This theme comes over a chromatic bass pedal effect, and sounds
rather weak against such ominous growling; hence it seems to fit
the description, especially as it enters here for the first time,
shortly before the end of the movement, and is given no development beyond its short duration of a little more than ten bars.

The second movement has even less actual following of the
score. The fugue subject is represented, with the increasing complication occasioned by the entry of more and more voices, in
lines 23-25, while the reference to waves which come closer and
closer, finally reaching the writer, may easily represent the passage leading up to the following theme, with the theme itself (bar
92) as the waves reach their goal:

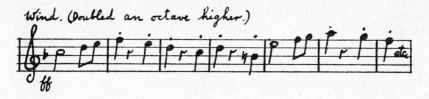

The philosophizing which follows cannot be directly connected with the music, though it is probable that the "Blitz und Donner" (line 36) refer to the passage (bar 186, ff.) where the kettledrums crash in every third bar with the predominant rhythmic theme of the movement. Possibly the "färb'ge Punkte" of line 40 refers to the theme of the *Trio,* taken by oboes and clarinets against a contrapuntal figure in the bassoon, and, if this is the case, the last two lines will indicate its repetition, in a high register, just before the three concluding bars of "thunder and lightning." It is probable, however, that this levitation is merely Plattensteiner's way of expressing the state of mind aroused by the music, and is not an attempt to suggest any particular part of it. He uses a similar figure in describing the first movement of the *Kreutzer Sonata,*[7] where there is certainly nothing in the score to indicate such an effect.

The third movement is described almost entirely in visual imagery chosen with a view to giving an impression of deep peace and contentment. There is no attempt to follow the form, which is that of a theme and variations, alternating with a theme which remains relatively unchanged, and there is no way of knowing why the poet chose the images here used in preference to any others which would give an effect of peace. The only specific reference to the music is found in lines 66-70, which refer to the sudden entry (bar 120) of a heavily accented theme for the full orchestra, in strong contrast with what has gone before. This theme returns at bar 130, and this time sinks to peace (as the poem remarks) by means of a note held over, diminuendo, by a horn, after the rest of the orchestra has dropped it. The three final lines on this movement are interesting in that they refer to the choral part in the following movement, although there is no hint of such a finale in the music at this point. This reference to what is to come fits in well with the poet's ideas and is perhaps legitimate as regards musical interpretation: in a familiar work, knowledge of what is to come certainly affects one's understand-

ing of what is actually in progress. However, this adumbration of
the final movement does prove that Plattensteiner was not trying
literally to follow the course of the music throughout his poem.

The account of the *Finale* begins with a striking interpretation
of the opening bars, which consist of a discordant crash, followed
by a sort of fanfare, *presto*:

It is interesting to find that Ernst Lissauer has employed the same
figure in speaking of Beethoven's music:

> Die Mauern barsten vom Schall seiner Posaunen und Tuben,
> Die Steine, gemeisselt, gemörtelt, behauen zu Quadern,
> Wellten und wölbten sich, zersplissen von Rillen und Adern.[8]

> The walls burst with the noise of his trombones and tubas; the chiseled,
> mortared, square-hewn stones heaved and buckled, split to pieces by cracks
> and veins.

The 'cellos and contrabasses, coming in "selon le caractère d'un
Récitatif," provide the assurance that all is well. Here again a
knowledge of what is to come influences the interpretation, for the
fact that the basses have a theme later used for the initial recitative accounts for their being considered reassuring: to anyone
familiar with the music they are a promise of the vocal section to
come, but on a first hearing they might easily seem no less ominous
than the opening fanfare. This fanfare is repeated, but the repetition is not indicated in the poem. However, the repetition follows so directly on its first appearance that the whole may be considered as one episode.

The following lines (79-80) are a reference back to the second
movement (lines 21 and 31), and hence they may be an attempt
to bring into the verse the passage (bars 30-76) in which Beethoven

tries over a few bars of each of the first three movements, as though
looking for a subject for the *Finale,* and rejects each of them in
turn. There is, however, no reference to the similar use of the
other two movements; hence it is possible that Plattensteiner was
following his own thoughts rather than attending to anything in
the music. He next gives out his "hohes Lied," the great choral
theme. It is first hinted at by four bars of prelude in the oboes,
clarinets, and bassoons, over a horn pedal which may be represented by the rock on which the poet stands. It is received with
approbation by the entire orchestra, led by the 'cellos and basses
in another recitative passage, and these instruments then play the
entire theme through in unison. They are the "gute Geister"
(line 86) who first sing it softly, and the next three lines refer to
its repetitions, each time by a larger portion of the orchestra: when
the 'cellos and basses have finished their first announcement of
the theme the violas and 'cellos take it up, with contrapuntal accompaniment in the basses and bassoons; next, the first violins
take it, with accompaniment by all the instruments already present plus the second violins; finally, it is given out by the full
orchestra. Plattensteiner is deceptive here with his "unsichtbar
singt's mit der Chor." He uses this phrase either to give vaguely the
effect of the volume of sound produced by the full orchestra or to
suggest that the chorus, which is soon to have the same theme, is
mentally singing it with the orchestra. Lines 91-92, "but the rest
of you do not understand its meaning until words explain it,"
show conclusively that the chorus has not yet actually entered.
Line 93 refers to the repetition of the opening fanfare (bars 208-
215) immediately preceding the baritone recitative which introduces the vocal part. After this, as was to be expected, Plattensteiner gives himself entirely to the text, and the remaining lines
have several verbal echoes of it.

In this attempt to correlate the poem with the music we have
found a number of definite and unmistakable references, as well
as a quantity of more doubtful ones. It should be observed that
a casual reading of the poem gives a better effect than a careful
study of it, score in hand, since in a casual reading one is struck
by the obvious allusions to the music and is not troubled by the
more obscure and sometimes inaccurate ones. This poem contains
no attempt at imitation or description of the music. In fact, with
the exception of the synaesthesia of the "färb'gen Noten," the only
specifically musical reference is the inaccurate one to the chorus

where no chorus is heard. Plattensteiner's method here is almost
entirely one of interpretation, and he is about evenly divided between the visual imagery of lapping waves, green meadows, and
crashing walls and the moral allegory of joys and threats. In this
respect the poem is typical of his works on music.

Turning to Todhunter's poem on the "Appassionata," we find
a more careful following of the music and a more highly developed
system of moral allegory.

I.

Through night's vast voiceless gloom a Sibyl cries
To man's heart some apocalyptic word,
Which falters on her tongue; then wailing flies
Like an affrighted bird.

5 Again she vainly strives; then desolate
With faltering voice flies wailing through the gloom,
While from the abyss of night reverberate
Menacing notes of doom.

Yet back she comes once more; but not alone,
10 For from the secret mountain solitude
Where thought's rebellious thunders have their home
She calls the Titan brood.

From earth to heaven they shout her prophecy,
While the fates laugh. Then all things listen mute:
15 With eager iterance flutter to the sky
Notes from a preluding flute.

Then from the awakened heart, on valorous wing,
A theme ardent as youth leaps joyously;
But in bold flight falls, as a wounded thing
20 Into a raging sea.

A Swan, a Royal Bark, it fights the waves
Of sudden storm. Wild voices throng the gale,
As in the rent clouds, while the vexed sea raves,
Contending spirits wail.

25 Voices of comfort, menace, or despair,
Answering the baffled theme, the Sibyl's cry,
Make, as they rise from ocean, earth, and air,
Tempestuous harmony.

O Swan! O Sibyl! with what remorseless foes,
30 Fate and Life's mocking winds, do ye contend,

And the unfathomed sea whose waves are woes,
With what far God for friend?

Fiercer the fight grows, louder shrieks the blast,
Long gusts of tempest, buffeting the Bark,
35 Drown the sad Sibyl's cry, and Hope, aghast,
Waits for the end. But hark!

Unvanquished still that jubilant song is heard,
Triumphing o'er the furious waves — once more
Fitfully sounds the Sibyl's cryptic word,
40 Clear through the tempest's roar.

In vain! The Swan-song strives with wearier note,
The unwearied waves bay like the hounds of doom,
The staggering Ship, o'erwhelmed, scarce keeps afloat,
Foundering in the gloom.

45 The old fight is fought, the tragic hour is past,
Sung is the saga of him who fate defies,
Magnificently strives, and foiled at last,
Magnificently dies.

O dauntless theme, O Swan, O Royal Ship,
50 O passion of our hearts! what comes to thee
In that last agony in the tempest's grip —
Defeat, or victory?

II.

Three chords, and all the world is listening,
Three chords, the hoary prophets of the key,
55 Their stern and solemn chant begin to sing,
Our hearts march to its tune, defying destiny.

Is it a dirge for some young hero dead,
Or a great hymn, hailing a god reborn
In a vexed age with doubts disquieted,
60 The dawn-song of a faith's new resurrection morn?

With the firm tread of a scarred veteran host
Retired from a disastrous field, but soon
Rallying to regain the vantage lost,
It marches calmly on — all hearts march to its tune.

65 It is the martyr's hymn of seers who lead
The world's Hope Forlorn: the resolute ecstasy
Of men who trust the faith for which they bleed
Burns in it as it breathes grave challenge to the sky.

      With slow majestic pace, as when the sun,
70 Gone down in tempest, through the eastern gate
      Unhurrying, tarrying not, his way has won,
      And fills all heaven with light, it marches calm as fate.

      Then faster throbs the music's pulse; the tramp
      Of the thin squadron falls with eagerer beat
75 As though, descried afar, the hostile camp
      With a quick thought of onset fired the marching feet.

      And now young spirits of joy ensky the theme
      In jubilant divisions as they sing,
      Their pinions flaming in the dawn's first gleam:
80 News of a hope new-born to earth from heaven they bring.

      Music, the day's bright voice, makes earth and air
      Palpitate in the divine invincible glee
      Of the glad choir's evangel, and despair
      Crouches, a spectre dumb in that vast symphony,

85 And ever more intense the sun's delight
      Flames in the rapture of each golden tone,
      Till the blithe spirits vanish in lingering flight,
      And the stern martyr's hymn is heard on earth alone.

      A judgment trumpet for the souls of men
90 It seems, as now the solemn chords outring,
      Ere seeking a full close, it sinks: and then
      Discords, like sudden clash of swords encountering!

III.

      And now, without a pause, inevitably
      We are swept onward, breathless, borne afar
95 By the swift-rushing steeds of phantasy
      To what strange land, vexed by what ghostly war?

      New tempest swoops over the desolate waste,
      Blurred by the twilight, trampled by the storm;
      Gust follows gust with fierce relentless haste,
100 And all familiar things have changed their form.

      Like a lithe wrestler, on the groaning earth
      The insistent gale hurls all its tyrannous weight,
      The new-born stars are smothered in their birth,
      The wind's will overbears our souls like fate.

105 And through the gloom a voice comes fitfully,
      In tones of anguish the rude gusts o'ercrow,

As of one worn with long calamity,
Pursued by some inexorable woe.

A hero's heart might break in that lone cry,
110 Too weak to rally his lost comrades — dead,
Or scattered like the leaves compelled to fly
Before the conquering blasts discomfited.

In a stern mood this epic scroll was penned,
The voice faints like a warrior's dying moan;
115 The tragic tale speeds swiftly to its end,
The exulting storm raves o'er the waste alone.

* * *

From what imperious fire, aching within
Outleaped this glowing lava of the heart?
By what long penance did this wizard win
120 From the witch Life the secret of her art?

Or did he boldly storm her palace gate,
And woo from her own hand her wand of power
Whereon the lightning's fiery shuttles wait,
Weaving a universe to mould a flower.

125 Ask, while the mighty music surges by,
Borne on the tempest's wing; from passion's deep
Summoning great visions to the inward eye,
And quickening thoughts that rouse the soul from sleep.

This poem follows the opening bars of the sonata with such exactness that there is no difficulty, at first, in correlating the verse and the music line by line and bar by bar. The first two lines correspond to the first three bars, and the wailing flight is in the last two bars of the excerpt:

The second stanza reproduces the repetition of this phrase, a semi-
tone higher, and the last two bars (the "flight") are twice repeated,
on different degrees of the scale, while a bass figure, the "menacing
notes of doom," comes between the repetitions, and is developed
after them, leading to a cadenza. Here we see the power of suggestion in producing an interpretation even so abstract as the general
conception of doom. Since many critics have commented on the
similarity between this theme (a) and the opening motif of
Beethoven's *Fifth Symphony* (b) which he himself is supposed to

have identified as the knock of fate at the door, it is extremely
probable that Todhunter was thinking of this similarity when he
interpreted the phrase as "doom."

The third attempt of the Sibyl, accompanied by the Titan
brood, is a repetition of the subject after the cadenza, but this
time it is broken up, and between the fragments are inserted bars
of fortissimo chords which shout their prophecy "from earth to
heaven" by the simple device of letting the left hand repeat the
chord unchanged, while the right hand goes up through its different positions.

Lines 15-16 are puzzling. Naturally, there can be and is no flute in a piano sonata, and we must suppose that the effect of such phrases as the following (bars 28-30) simply seemed flute-like to the poet.

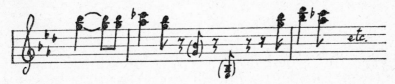

This brings us to the second subject (bar 36, ff.), "a theme ardent as youth":

Its fall into a raging sea (lines 19-20) is accomplished by means of a phrase reminiscent of the flight of the Sibyl's word, leading to three bars of rising trills, and then to a run which descends four and a half octaves "into a raging sea" of accompaniment. At this point visual imagery enters in, and what had been merely a theme becomes "a Swan, a Royal Bark" as it rides the storm accompaniment:

Todhunter has now reached the point (reached sooner or later by all who attempt to follow the larger musical forms with poetic description or imitation) where the utmost efforts of verse are powerless to deal with the increasing complication of the music, which is here entering upon the development section. Music can change themes in many ways and keep them recognizable, but in poetry such variation is extremely difficult, and is more likely to lead to a feeling of tautology than to any semblance of develop-

ment. Also, the outstanding difference between music and poetry,
so far as technique is concerned, here comes into play: poetry can
say only one thing at a time, whereas music can combine themes
indefinitely. It may have been this difficulty which made Todhunter resort to visual imagery in order to present the idea of
the theme and its stormy accompaniment existing and progressing
simultaneously. (Alice Meynell uses an identical figure to describe the melody floating on the "accompaniment" in the Bach-
Gounod *Ave Maria*.)

At any rate, with line 25 he relinquishes the attempt to follow
the music in detail, and begins to generalize about the development section, using the standard metaphor of a struggle to express
the combining and conflicting themes. In passing, we may note
the debt to Shelley in line 31; much poetry of this type is largely
derivative. There are still occasional references to the music, but
the attempt to take it consecutively has had to be abandoned. The
Sibyl's cry of line 35 is the initial theme, in a changed form, entering at bar 66, and the reappearance of "that jubilant song"
(line 37) is the re-entry of the second subject at bar 110. The
Sibyl's theme enters again at bar 136 and "fitfully sounds" (line
39) until bar 174, but this time there is no mention of the "Titan
brood," although in bar 153 they reappear in much their original
form. This omission may be due to the fact that the description
has now become more general, but it is interesting to notice that,
since the Sibyl's cry is supposed to be sounding fitfully and more
or less despairingly here, it will not do to call attention to the
passage in which it returns with all its original strength. The "in
vain!" of line 41 would be pointless if the Titan brood were re-
introduced into the story. The Swan-song "strives with wearier
note" because it is a third lower at its next appearance, if the
second subject is meant, but there seems to be some confusion
between the second subject and the theme which appeared at its
fall into the sea. Todhunter apparently treats them as identical.
From this point on he abandons the music entirely and follows
out the interpretation which he has begun, carrying his allegory
to its logical conclusion. If the ardent theme of bar 36 rises on
valorous wing and then falls into the sea, it repeats the performance in bars 175-191, but we hear no mention of this fact; the
theme continues to be a ship, which ultimately founders. At the
close of this section the moral allegory is driven home by identifi-
cation of the ship as the "passion of our hearts."

The second movement is a set of variations on a double theme, and no attempt is made to follow the music so closely as at the beginning of the first movement. The opening notes (the triads of the tonic and subdominant, with a return to the tonic) are

described as "three chords, the hoary prophets of the key" — a phrase which would normally lead us to expect a progression of tonic to subdominant to dominant. The exact connection between the first five stanzas and the music cannot be determined. The music consists of four divisions: a theme is given out in two well-defined sections, and a variation on each of these follows. Each of the four divisions is repeated once, and it is impossible to fit the five stanzas to the four musical sections with any certainty.

We find ourselves again at "then faster throbs the music's pulse" (line 73), for this phrase certainly refers to the variation in sixteenth notes, and the apparent acceleration is given a programmatic explanation. The variations in thirty-second notes are young spirits of joy (lines 77-87), and the obsolete technical term *divisions* is used. As a rule Todhunter avoids specifically technical terms, but this one has a literary pedigree and is obsolete; hence it is not too prosaic for poetical use. The average reader would probably consider it merely a vague word used by poets in writing of music, and would not suspect it of being a technical word used with absolute accuracy. After these variations the thirty-second notes "vanish in lingering flight" — they run down the scale and into the bass for a repetition of the original theme. After a few bars of this theme the second movement leads directly into the third. "Seeking a full close, it sinks" in what we expect to be a final cadence: Ii, I, V₇ii, Ii, I, IIi, V — "and then discords, like sudden clash of swords encountering!" — instead of the expected final tonic chord we have, first *pianissimo* and then *fortissimo*, the diminished seventh chord of the new key, F minor.

"And now, without a pause, inevitably, we are swept onward." The *Finale* follows immediately, keeping the same "discord" for its first five bars. This movement is followed even less closely than the preceding one. The "tempest" enters immediately after the five introductory bars:

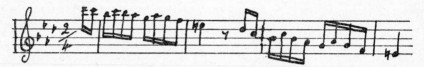

It is *allegro non troppo,* and is immediately repeated an octave lower. Beyond this "tempest," however, we can identify nothing, for the movement is described in very general terms. "A voice comes fitfully" (line 105) almost throughout the entire movement, and we cannot say just where "that lone cry" (line 109) is to be found. More interesting still is the fact that there is no recognizable mention of the remarkable *Presto* shortly before the end. In reading this poem one is forced to the conclusion that the poet grew weary and discouraged in his attempt to follow the music closely, and that he finally more or less abandoned it and shifted his attention to his own moral allegory.

The foregoing analysis shows how musical elements are translated into both visual imagery and moral personifications. Todhunter frequently combines the two: a theme can be at the same time merely a joyous song, a swan or a ship *ad libitum,* and a symbol of beauty and heroism at war with an adverse fate. The little epilogue of three stanzas suggests interpretation in terms of the composer's life, and sums up the musical effects which we have noticed throughout the poem: for Todhunter music produces both visions and abstract moral ideas, "from passion's deep/ Summoning great visions to the inward eye,/ And quickening thoughts that rouse the soul from sleep." There seems also to be some allegory of time.[9] The first movement is at night (lines 1 and 44); the second lasts from dawn to about noon and several times compares the music to the course of the sun; and the last takes place at twilight (lines 98, 103, and 105).

Edgar Lee Masters' poem *Beethoven's Ninth Symphony and the King Cobra* is unusual in that it employs practically all the methods of musical description and interpretation, and it is of particular interest in that it gives us an opportunity to study the use of critical and biographical source-material in musical poetry.

Since it is a long philosophical poem, those parts dealing with the music will here be placed together, with the omissions indicated by asterisks. The central idea of the poem is that life traps matter into individual consciousness, holding the individual off from the rest of the world and giving him the power to feel, and hence to suffer.

* * *

95 But Beethoven, so evoked after long aeons,
   Is he not evil, too?
   Is he truth and beauty, yet a sufferer, and producing suffering?
   Is he truth and beauty, who awakens greater consciousness?
   Or is he continued evil, bringing pain and despair,
100 And deeper looks into the nothingness whence we came,
   And a forecast of the resumption of sleep whither we tend?
   Is he then evil as he shows these things to the full?
   Does he not disturb us, as he does the cobra,
   Which crawls and writhes and lifts itself
105 As it hears Beethoven through oboes
   Tell of his sorrows and sufferings,
   The neglect that the world heaped upon him,
   His poverty and loneliness,
   Loneliness as lonely as this glass-cage of the cobra;
110 All of which Beethoven uttered in music, and in the cry:
   "I have no friend,
   "I am alone in the world.
   "O God, my Rock, my All,
   "Thou Unutterable, hear Thy unhappy,
   "Thy most unhappy of mortals."

* * *

   It is more than a hundred years past and gone
205 Since Beethoven cried:
   "God, O God, my Guardian, my Rock, my All!
   "Thou seest my heart, and knowest how it distresses me
   "To do harm to others, though doing right to my darling Karl.
   "Hear, Thou Unutterable, hear Thy unhappy,
210 "Most unhappy of mortals:
   "I have no friend, and am alone in the world!"

   Shall this cry never die out?
   Never be hushed as the crackling of weeds is hushed
   After the giant thunder-lizard has walked on?
215 Shall it never vanish as the rib-marks of the serpent in the sand
   Are erased by the wind?
   It is more than a hundred years now since Beethoven
   Set down his misery and his ecstasy,

His wounded and baffled spirit,
220 His climbing and sun-lit and triumphant spirit
In dots and curves, in numerals and time signatures,
In key signatures, in breves and semi-breves,
In major and minor keys, and ledger lines and clefs,
In bars of duple, triple and quadruple time, in rests and scales,
225 In indications for winds and strings,
Flutes, horns, bassoons and viols —
All set down, and all to say in harmony:
Alone! Alone! Alone!
All set down so to direct forever the players of instruments
230 How to pass from the earthquake rumble of the lost city of the soul
To the sunlight and song of the safe slopes;
How to pass with whisperings and falterings,
Almost as of children in fear,
To fathomless depths of courage and wisdom;
235 How to pace the harmony of the going-out,
And the returning-in of the Universe,
When the heart of the Great Law opens and closes its valves.
And how with plucked strings of summoned courage,
And the clamor of drums, to climb, to stand
240 Where no cobra crawls, no devil walks,
No charms of hell are worked;
And where the silence of a great summit
Opens out as a flower trembles and unfolds
Revealing the drone of spheres, the song, the infinite music
245 Of light, which is also sound,
And which is impulse at the root of all motion,
And which is without end in space or time.

It is more than a hundred years since the secrets
Of Beethoven's soul, of his vision,
250 Were noted on paper in these cryptograms.
Yet, and because this was done
Beethoven's suffering and rapture reverberate still. . . .
                                        * * *

This is the way Beethoven entered the cage of the cobra:
The next day after the seven-fold scale was removed,
300 The next day after the cobra swallowed the gopher-snake,
The Ninth Symphony was played in the Park;
And the keeper turned on the radio in the reptile room
To see what the cobra would do,
When the sounds of the Scherzo and the Ode to Joy
305 Echoed and re-echoed about the stone walls.
                                        * * *

As the musicians at the Park took the soul of Beethoven
320 From the dots, dashes, signs and symbols of score sheets,

And gave it voice as lettered there, forever sealed, and forever
    unsealed at will
As the echo of Beethoven's soul echoing the Great Mystery
    somewhere,
Not as an imitation of Nature, or of anything in Nature,
But as a response to Something,
325 Even as the agitation of the cobra is a response to Beethoven!

The second violins and cellos, the first violins, tenors and basses
Begin to whisper their way from the top to the bottom of the
    treble stave
To the bottom of the bass.
A clarinet breaks in like the call of a lonesome summer bird;
330 And one by one the wind-instruments enter,
And then the flutes and oboes divide the lamentation,
They are saying: "God, O God, my Guardian,
"My Rock, my All! Hear Thou, Unutterable,
"Hear Thy unhappy, most unhappy of mortals!"
                  * * *

The Scherzo changes all.
370 Beethoven's soul stepped from darkness to brilliant light,
From despair to the rapture of strength,
Overcoming the world.
Beethoven caught the spirit of a fresh May morning,
And it inspired him to exult with trumpets and strings,
375 And drums and trombones.
There are no such mornings in the jungle.
The rhythm of three bars changed to the rhythm of four bars
Is nothing less than the secret ecstasy of May;
It is nothing less than the thrill of life,
380 Making the worm feel the blisses of creation,
And making man himself a dweller with Eternity.

And now this ecstatic storm of harmony
Is not only the voices of strong men,
And the creak of great pulleys worked by them
385 To lift colossal blocks of granite to the terraces
Of timeless pyramids;
It is not merely discords resolved:
It is not the mere toppling and crash of colossi,
Followed by the silence of Egyptian palm groves;
390 It is not merely the audible silence
Which comes before the hollow sound,
And is followed by the hollow silence
When covers are lifted and placed on great earthen jars
Which have been filled with water for thirsty villages.
395 It is not merely the trumpeting of mastodons
Amid carboniferous thickets,

Or along the level valleys of lava and giant cactus —
It is not merely these,
Nor merely Democritus laughing and shouting as he chases the
    discovered atom
400 Near the orbit of Uranus where time and space become one;
It is not merely any of these.
But it is the song of infinite cranes
Lifting worlds into their orbits;
It is the deep sighing of aeons of time;
405 It is the chuckle of vast ages;
It is the puffing and halloos of periodic cycles
Toiling up the spirals of infinitude;
It is the sound of smooth-lipped lids of crystal
Being placed on huge vials of despair and fear,
410 After their bitter waters have been poured into the flaming rivers
Of all old Hells, to the roar of steam.
It is the sound of ponderable slabs
Being laid and fitted to the sarcophagi of dead demi-gorgons;
It is the happy laughter from the cradle of the infant Heracles
415 As he strangled the snakes sent by the enmity of Hera;
It is the shout of Heracles despising the common kingdom
Of which Hera, the jealous goddess, deprived him.
It is the howl of fire from worlds which should be burned,
Amid the drift and swirl of apocalyptic smoke;
420 It is the splash of the lake of fire
When death is hurled down and engulfed;
It is the thunder of mountain-high gates being opened,
Which reveal the landscapes of eternity;
It is the shout and the song of Apollo
425 As he races and shoots arrows after fleeing dragons.
It is the chant of the Sun as god of this world,
Worthy of worship as the source of life!

Let us begin our examination of this poem with the description of the opening bars of the symphony (lines 326-334). We find an unusually musicianly account of this passage. The reference to the top of the treble and the bottom of the bass stave fixes the compass of the phrase accurately, and few indeed are the poets who make a distinction between first and second violins. These things alone are sufficient reason for suspecting that the author, not being a professional musician, decided to write a philosophical poem on this subject, and, knowing what blunders literary men often make in their attempts to deal with music, decided to go to some authority for his musical information. Turning now to Sir George Grove's *Beethoven and his Nine Symphonies,* we find the following description of the same passage:[10]

All is pianissimo; the second violins and cellos sound the accompaniment, with the horns in unison, to give it more consistency, while the first violins, tenors, and basses are heard successively whispering their way through them from the top of the treble stave to the bottom of the bass — still, however, avoiding the third of the chord: —

This is repeated, after a bar's interval, with the difference that the first violins begin on the upper A instead of on the E, and that a clarinet is added to the accompaniment; and then the phrase is given a third time, but with a very Beethovenish difference: the intervals remain the same, but the phrase is hurried — twice, the second time more hurried than the first. And so, at last, the wind instruments coming in one by one, and the whole increasing in force bar by bar, we are launched. . . .

Here we find most of the elements used by Masters: the reference to "whispering" and to the position of the notes on the staves, the viola called by the not-too-common name of *tenor,* the reference to the clarinet in particular, and the general statement that the wind instruments enter *one by one.* There can be no possible doubt that Masters took his description from Grove and followed his original closely. The only point in which he really modified or added to his original was the insertion of the phrase "like the call of a lonesome summer bird" to describe the clarinet, and it has been previously noted that, although this may be very effective for a reader, it gives a false impression of the musical effect which it seeks to describe.

"The flutes and oboes divide the lamentations" in the second subject,[11] of which Grove says: "It begins with a *legato* phrase, in three members of two bars each, divided between the flutes, oboes, and clarinets."[12] However, Masters seems to have taken his interpretation of it from a hint on a theme late in the movement. (See p. 116, second musical quotation.) Of this passage Grove writes:[13]

Was ever grief at once more simply, more fully, and more touchingly told? The sorrows which wounded the great composer during so many of the last

years of his life, through his deafness, his poverty, his sensitiveness, his bodily
sufferings, the annoyances of business, the ingratitude and rascality of his
nephew, the slights of friends, the neglect of the world — sorrows on which
he kept silence, except for a few words in his letters, are here beheld in all
their depth and bitterness. Surely if anywhere he has here produced his
proprio e proposto effetto.

We find that Masters took his biographical interpretation as
well as his musical description from Grove, for a careful reading
of his complete article on the *Ninth Symphony,* including the biographical discussion of its period, reveals that practically everything dealing with music in Masters' poem comes from this source.
The poem uses letters, diaries, and remarks of other critics, but
the way in which they are used indicates that all of them are taken
from Grove's article.

In giving the biographical background of this symphony Grove
writes:[14]

The following entry is still more touching, and is a good specimen of the
way in which his [Beethoven's] inmost being was rent and racked at this
period of his life. It dates from the early part of 1818: 'God, O God, my
Guardian, my Rock, my All, Thou seest my heart, and knowest how it distresses me to do harm to others through doing right to my darling Karl. Hear
Thou, unutterable! hear Thy unhappy, most unhappy of mortals.' 'I have
no friend,' he says to Fräulein del Rio at this time, 'and am alone in the
world.'

Masters takes this passage over bodily, the only change being that
of "through doing right" to "though doing right," and the fact
that he makes a single quotation of these two extracts from different sources shows conclusively that he took them from Grove,
where they occur together. The "Alone! Alone! Alone!" of line
228 also comes from a letter quoted by Grove.[15]

Even when Masters turns to general, non-biographical interpretation he still proceeds cautiously and on authority — on several
authorities, in fact, but all available in Grove. These authorities
are, however, used with considerable freedom. Grove's statement
that the *Scherzo* is founded upon "one single phrase of three notes,
which is said to have come suddenly into Beethoven's mind as
he stepped from darkness into brilliant light"[16] is used figuratively
in the poem:

> Beethoven's soul stepped from darkness to brilliant light,
> From despair to the rapture of strength,
> Overcoming the world.

Berlioz is treated with even greater freedom, for his remark about a May morning (quoted by Grove[17]) was originally applied to the effect of the oboe in the trio of the *Scherzo*, between bar 454 and bar 475. Masters uses it to apply to the change in the rhythm of the fugue subject to "ritmo di tre battute" at bar 177 and back again to "ritmo di quattro battute" at bar 233:

> The rhythm of three bars changed to the rhythm of four bars
> Is nothing less than the secret ecstasy of May;
> It is nothing less than the thrill of life,
> Making the worm feel the blisses of creation,
> And making man himself a dweller with Eternity.

This passage also shows that use of the text for interpretation which is so inevitable in any poem dealing with vocal music: though Masters does not go beyond the *Scherzo* he here brings in a part of the *Finale*, and shows a last reliance on his source, the form of the allusion revealing that it was taken from the translation of Schiller's ode in Grove.[18] The extremes which come together in this passage are interesting: Berlioz' statement about a later and quite different part of the movement is taken as the main subject, and this is enlarged on by an allusion to the verse of Schiller to which Beethoven gave a musical setting in the last movement of the symphony.

Nevertheless, the effect is good. So also is that of the concluding passage, which seems to be largely Masters' own idea and is an elaboration of his earlier statement that the symphony is to be taken

> Not as an imitation of Nature, or of anything in Nature,
> But as a response to Something.

This final statement takes the point of view of the moral allegorists, saying that music is not an expression of anything objective, or of any specific event, but rather an expression of universal forces. We might even call it an example of imitation of music in that the long period in which this idea is developed, with all its parallel phrases, its two great sections of things which the music is not and things which it is, and the parallelism of the ideas in the two groups, has something of the structure and a great deal of the effect of a symphonic passage.

In this poem Masters has succeeded in the difficult task of making a musical composition live for his readers, and he has succeeded by the apparently unpromising method of using musical analysis and the strange device of description of the score (we now understand why he used it) to give his readers some idea of the music itself before he sets about interpreting it. His interpretation is biographically accurate, even if we do find a somewhat sentimentalized Beethoven in it. Up to this point he has stuck to his authorities, probably not feeling at home on strictly musical ground. Now, however, when he comes to the matter of interpretation, he accepts hints and suggestions from them, but does not consider them binding. His interpretation does not use any concrete scenes which we might be inclined to dispute if they were contrary to our own visualizations, or if we had none: "Beethoven caught the *spirit* of a fresh May morning," but "there are no such mornings in the jungle."[19] In the passage telling what the music is not he manages to suggest a great many possibilities, and thus to satisfy those who think of music in terms of visual imagery, without giving any of them as the true interpretation. There are few musical enthusiasts indeed who would refuse him, in a poem, the right to interpret a symphony in terms of the vast and vague powers which he uses. Perhaps the most important thing of all for the final effect is the fact that he manages, in the verse of his last passage, to give us something of the effect of hearing great music. All these elements combine to make this poem the most successful attempt at a poetic treatment of a musical composition which has been found in the course of this study.

CHAPTER **VIII** : Final Judgments

Our discussion has been based primarily on about three hundred poems* which make some attempt to deal with specific musical compositions in a poetic way. Since there is no one method of finding material of this type, it is a certainty that a number of similar poems have been overlooked, but since the search covered several years of browsing in large libraries and reading in authors interested in the relations between music and poetry, I feel that the material is various and plentiful enough to be fully representative. That some poems have been neglected is certain, but that any element of importance in the poetical use of musical compositions has been overlooked is doubtful. Not nearly all the poems illustrative of any given point could be quoted in the foregoing study, but they have all been taken into consideration in forming general conclusions.

Having studied the methods used by the poetic transcribers of music, we may well ask ourselves what literary value their works have, apart from their interest for students of music and aesthetics. It must be admitted that, with a few exceptions, most of the writers represented in this study are distinctly minor figures, and are practically unknown in literature. They belong to the mushroom crop of poets who publish a few books of verse, gain, per-

---

*There would be no point in trying to make a pedantically exact count. The estimate here exceeds the number of items listed in the Bibliography because some poets, like Gregh and Godoy, have written separate poems for each musical number of a group. Thus their works on Schumann's *Carnival* actually consist of twenty poems each.

137

haps, some little attention and praise, and are shortly confined to the dusty stacks of large libraries and the dark corners of second-hand bookshops, whence they issue forth only when some particular study calls them out for a few moments. Most of them are definitely "dated," though a few hang on in certain places: an Australian friend informed me that he was brought up on the works of Frances Ridley Havergal. Nevertheless, it may certainly be said that many of them are as good as some of our highly praised contemporary poets will seem twenty-five years hence.

Also, among much mechanical versification we find occasional flashes of poetry, and among many mediocre poems we find some excellent ones. It is not the purpose of this study to go into detailed criticism of anything except the use made of music in these poems, and we cannot attempt any lengthy account of the literary merits and faults of these productions apart from what is necessarily involved in the study of the effectiveness and accuracy with which the effect or form of music was reproduced. However, the reader will naturally have made criticisms for himself from the · numerous citations of verse scattered throughout the preceding chapters, and will be in a position to form his own estimate of the literary value of these works.

When we come to the question of how far poets can reproduce or suggest music in their verse, we are forced to rely almost entirely on the preceding chapters, for few critics have dealt with the question. Albert Gehring's *The Basis of Musical Pleasure*[1] develops the thesis that music is, as has often been remarked, the art of thinking in tones; but Gehring carries out the idea in detail, showing that the standard devices of musical development are similar to the processes of logical thought. Since poetry is for the most part the particularly apt expression of thought, if we accept Gehring's theory we are forced to the conclusion that poetry and music are governed by identical laws. However, there is one distinction of great importance: the sounds and groups of sounds used in poetry have all a conventional and arbitrary significance attached to them, and hence poetical thought deals with external objects and concepts. Music, on the other hand, is pure sound. If we except such occasional devices as the Wagnerian *Leitmotiv,* music is sound moving only in accordance with its own laws. Thus we may say that any verbal meaning found in music is usually put there by the interpreter. Proust is illuminating on this point. He writes:

Persuadé que les œuvres que j'entendais (au concert symphonique) expri-
maient les vérités les plus hautes, je tâchais de m'élever autant que je le
pouvais, pour atteindre jusqu'à elles, je tirais de moi, pour les comprendre,
je leur remettais tout ce que je recélais alors de meilleur, de plus profond.[2]

Convinced that the works which I heard (at the symphony concerts) expressed the highest verities, I tried to exalt myself as far as I could in order
to attain to their level; in order to understand them, I drew out from myself
and put into them all that was then best and deepest in me.

This is an open confession that Proust found the meaning in himself and inserted it into the music.

Hanslick's famous figure of speech compares music to a moving
arabesque. One would hardly ask the meaning of an arabesque,
though he might well demand to know the significance of a picture. The arabesque and the picture may well represent music
and poetry: the figures in a painting have a significance independent of their form and color, while those in an arabesque are pure
form used for its own sake. If this analogy is to hold good, however, we must assume that the arabesque makes up for its lack
of objective significance by being able to produce far more rich,
varied, and complicated graphic effects than are possible in the
painting.

This is not to say that music is too vague to be put into words,
but that its significance is of a different sort from that of speech:
the two means of expression are, mathematically speaking, incom-
mensurable. Mendelssohn explained this fact in a famous letter[3]
to Marc André Souchay, who had assigned names to a number of
the *Songs Without Words,* and had written to Mendelssohn to ask
whether his names were correct. The point of Mendelssohn's illuminating reply is that music is too definite to be put into
words — that it has a definiteness of a different kind.

Das, was mir eine Musik ausspricht, die ich liebe, sind mir nicht zu *un-
bestimmte* Gedanken, um sie in Worte zu fassen, sondern zu *bestimmte.* So
finde ich in allen Versuchen, diese Gedanken auszusprechen, etwas Richtiges,
aber auch in allen etwas Ungenügendes, und so geht es mir auch mit den
Ihrigen.

A piece of music which I love expresses to me ideas which are not too *indefinite* to be put into words, but rather too *definite.* Therefore in all attempts
to state these ideas I find some rightness, but also something unsatisfactory,
and I feel this about yours also.

This is as complete an answer as can be given on theoretical grounds.

From the practical point of view of this investigation, the question of how far poets have actually been able to reproduce or suggest specific pieces of music in their verse has already been answered piecemeal. We may sum up the results by saying that those who rely entirely on interpretation have no success whatsoever, and only by some technical description of the score, orchestration, harmony, or other specifically musical features can the reader be given any idea of the music. Let anyone who questions this statement turn to some of the numerous poems which interpret music without describing or identifying it, and attempt to identify the compositions himself. Plattensteiner's *Quartett; Opus Nummer ?*[4] and *Frühlingssymphonie*,[5] which he annotates as "Träumerei in Worten vom Inhalt einer Sonata," are good examples. We know that these poems refer to a Beethoven quartette and a Beethoven sonata respectively, but it is absolutely impossible to say to which quartette and to which sonata. It is significant that the greater poets have not, as a rule, given us interpretations of this kind. Either they tell us what the composition is and assume a familiarity with the music as a basis for comments on the composer or on art in general, as did Grillparzer; or, if they attempt any interpretation of the music, they first identify the piece in question and provide enough technical or at least specifically musical description of it to give the reader an idea of the composition itself on which to hang any interpretation which may follow. Browning is an example of this latter method.

After we have thus been informed as to what the music is, we may sometimes find an interpretation of it pleasing and felicitous. Schumann reports that when a young composer wished to read him the program of a composition before playing it, he said: "Vor allem lass mich hören, dass du schöne Musik gemacht, hinterher soll mir auch dein Programm angenehm sein."[6] ("First of all let me hear that you have composed beautiful music; after that, your program too will interest me.") The same thing might be said to the interpretive poets. They should first tell us about the music, or, if they wish to write pure interpretation without treating the music on which it is based, they should merely present their works as philosophical or descriptive poems, instead of irritating and puzzling us by interpreting a music of which we can know nothing. If these principles are followed, poets can obtain fairly satisfactory results in the poetic interpretation of music, although they can never give more than a bare idea of the music itself. In this respect Schumann's young composer had the advantage: he could play his music before he gave the program. Perhaps, however, it is this inadequacy of words thoroughly to express music, even technically, which makes the poets consider some interpretation necessary. We have already seen one witness who testified that any attempt to interpret music in words is a more or less conscious imposture, and it may well be true that many poets who listen to music analytically feel the necessity of falling back on interpretation when they wish to deal with it verbally.

Finally, I shall state my personal convictions on the matter of the meaning of music, in order that a due discount may be made for any prejudices which may have crept into the discussion. It has been my constant attempt to avoid any bias, and the fact that my ideas on musical aesthetics have undergone considerable change under the influence of the material for this study is evidence of reasonable success. However, it is certain that persons whose imagery is predominantly auditory (the analytic listeners) and those who think in terms of visual imagery (the hearers who see pictures) can never fully understand each other. The characterizers of music as joyous or sad and the moral allegorists stand halfway between these two extremes. It is my personal conviction that the description of music in terms of visual images *which have no characteristic sound associated with them* is doomed to utter failure, while its description in terms of thunder, brooks, rustling leaves, etc., is possible, but is, as Dryden would say, "needless curiosity." These remarks apply, of course, only to "absolute" music; if the composer has given us a program for his work the poet certainly cannot be condemned for following it, although, in spite of the composer's authority, he probably will not succeed particularly well in his poetic version. In the characterizers of music and the moral allegorists I see some meaning, though even here I should prefer a thorough exposition of the music before any interpretation is advanced. On the whole, and with a few definite exceptions, I find that poems dealing with music in any but specifically musical terms are unsatisfactory, and the use of musical terms to produce effective poetry is extremely difficult. My final opinion on the matter is, *mutatis mutandis,* that of Lessing on a poetic description of the Laocoön group:[7]

Ich begreife wohl, wie seine vor sich selbst arbeitende Phantasie ihn auf diesen und jenen Zug bringen können; aber die Ursachen, warum seine Beurteilungskraft schöne Züge, die er vor Augen gehabt, in diese andere Züge verwandeln zu müssen glaubte, diese wollen mir nirgends einleuchten.

I can see well enough how his independently working imagination might produce this or that trait; but the original reasons why his judgment felt called upon to change the beautiful traits which were before his eyes into other traits are beyond my comprehension.

It would be both unjust and inaccurate to close the discussion on such a depressing note without reminding the reader of the strict limitations of this study. The poem on a specific composition is, in general, inadequate and derivative. On the other hand, music has been an important source of inspiration and of techniques in recent literature, as can be readily seen in the works of such writers as Proust, Conrad Aiken, and Thomas Mann. The difference is that they use music for suggestions, for new literary devices, and for various types of special effects, whereas the poets with whom we have been concerned merely set out, not to create something of their own, but to translate the untranslatable.

Notes

◇

CHAPTER I

1. Théodore Gérold, *Les pères de l'Église et la musique* (Strasbourg, 1931), p. 178.
2. *Ibid.*, p. 179, note 1.
3. *Inferno,* XXXIV, 1.
4. *Orpheus and Eurydice,* II, 219-242.
5. Mary Jane Estcourt, *Music, the Voice of Harmony in Creation* (London, 1857), pp. 18-20.
6. For a general discussion of Ronsard's connections with music and his theories of musical art and poetry, see *Ronsard et la musique: numéro spécial de la Revue Musicale* (Paris, May 1, 1924). It contains a number of articles by different critics on various aspects of the subject.
7. *Melissi Schedismata Poetica, pars altera,* secundo edita multo auctiora (Paris, 1586), p. 88 ff.
8. *The Faerie Queene,* II, xii, 33.
9. E. W. Naylor, *Shakespeare and Music* (London, 1896).
10. Sigmund Spaeth, *Milton's Knowledge of Music; its Sources and its Significance in his Works* (Weimar, 1913).
11. *Paradise Lost,* XI, 557-559.
12. *L'Allegro,* pp. 139-144.
13. Thomas, *A History of German Literature* (N. Y., 1928), p. 177.
14. Avison, *An Essay on Musical Expression* (London, 1753), p. 117.
15. Grétry, *Mémoires ou essais sur la musique* (Brussels, 1829), III, 193.
16. Guerlac, *Les citations françaises* (Paris, 1931), p. 214.
17. See J. B. Weckherlin's *Nouveau Musiciana* (Paris, 1890).
18. The *Grub-Street Journal,* No. 280 (May 8, 1735).
19. Sonnets and score were originally published in Amsterdam, 1720. The poems are accessible in an English translation in the backs of the albums of the Concert Hall Society's recording (AR, I, II). The modern authoritative edition of Vivaldi's music, sponsored by the Instituto Italiano Antonio Vivaldi (Fascicles 76-79) unaccountably omits the sonnets.
20. *Ibid.*, pp. 72-73. A discussion of Gerstenberg's work, together with the music of Bach's Fantasia and Gerstenberg's texts, is available in the *Vierteljahrsschrift für Musikgeschichte,* 1891, Part I, pp. 5-14.
21. W. M. F. Petrie, *The Revolutions of Civilisation,* 3rd ed. (London, 1922).
22. Cecil Gray, *Predicaments, or Music and the Future* (London, 1936), Ch. III.
23. See Irving Babbitt, *The New Laokoon, an Essay on the Confusion of the Arts* (Boston & N. Y., 1910).
24. The idea goes back to Castel (1688-1757). For a general discussion see A. W. Rimington, *Colour-Music, the Art of Mobile Colour* (London, 1912).
25. A perfume-concert was given in New York in 1902. (Babbitt, *op. cit.,* p. 182.)
26. Huysmans, *A rebours* (Paris, 1905), pp. 62-64.
27. Zola, *Le ventre de Paris,* Chapter V.
28. Huber, *Böcklin Symphony;* Rachmaninoff, *Die Toteninsel;* Reger, *Der geigende Eremit, Im Spiel der Wellen, Die Toteninsel, Bacchanal;* Schulzbeuthen, *Die Toteninsel;* Weingartner, *Das Gefilde der Seligen.*
29. *Ludwig Tiecks sämmtliche Werke* (Wien, 1818), XIII, 213-220.
30. See A. Cœuroy, *Musique et littérature* (Paris, 1923), pp. 11-48.
31. *Herzensergiessungen eines kunstliebenden Klosterbruders: Phantasien über die Kunst für Freunde der Kunst* (Potsdam, 1925), p. 136.
32. *Ibid.*, pp. 158-163.
33. E. T. A. Hoffmann, *Kreisleriana* (Reklam), p. 34.
34. Cœuroy, *Musique et littérature,* p. 40.

35. See Eduard Hanslick, *Musikalische Stationen* (Berlin, 1880), pp. 331-361, and *Musikalisches und Litterarisches* (Berlin, 1889), pp. 269-278, for essays on Grillparzer's musical interests. See also Anna Wutzky, *Grillparzer und die Musik* (Regensburg, 1940).
36. *Grillparzers Werke* (Leipzig, 1903), I, 136-152.
37. Baldensperger, *Sensibilité musicale et romantisme* (Paris, 1925). This work and R. L. Evans, *Les romantiques français et la musique* (Paris, 1934), are the best accounts of the musical aspects of French romantic literature.
38. Baldensperger, *op. cit.*, p. 104.
39. George Sand, *La coupe, etc.* (Paris, 1876), pp. 261-298.
40. Gautier, *Émaux et camées*, 1852.
41. *Ibid.*
42. Evans, *op. cit.*, pp. 40-49.
43. Cœuroy, *Appels d'Orphée*, p. 148.
44. *Ibid.*, p. 150.
45. Cœuroy, *Musique et littérature*, pp. 21-22.
46. Wagner's influence on the novel is a large study in itself. See A. Cœuroy, *Appels d'Orphée*, pp. 197-214; Kurt Jäckel, *Richard Wagner in der französischen Literatur*, II (Breslau, 1932); Anna Jacobson, *Nachklänge Richard Wagners im Roman* (Heidelberg, 1932); Max Moser, *Richard Wagner in der englischen Literatur des XIX. Jahrhunderts* (Bern, 1938); Rosemary Park, *Das Bild von Richard Wagners Tristan und Isolde in der deutschen Literatur* (Jena, 1935).
47. *Complete Works and Letters of Charles Lamb* (N. Y., 1935), pp. 546-547.
48. *Blackwood's Edinburgh Magazine*, LXVI, No. 310 (December, 1849), pp. 750-755.
49. *The Poetical Works of Mrs. Felicia Hemans* (London, n. d.), pp. 461-463.
50. Estcourt, *op. cit.*
51. For information on Browning's actual competence, see Herbert E. Greene, "Browning's Knowledge of Music," *PMLA*, LXII, 1095-99.
52. Charles van den Borren, "Round About *A Toccata of Galuppi's*," *Musical Times & Singing-Class Circular*, May 1, 1923.
53. Section xlii.
54. Sections xci-xciii.
55. *The Poetical Works of Frances Ridley Havergal* (London, 1884), II, 23-29.
56. *Ibid.*, I, 11-19.
57. *Poezje Kornela Ujejskiego* (Lipsk, 1866).
58. Westminster, 1899.
59. N. Y., 1906.
60. London, 1905.
61. See Baldensperger, *La musique dans la littérature contemporaine* (Lyon, 1908).
62. Paris, 1897.
63. Paris, 1907.
64. Madeleine Merens-Melmer, *Sous la signe de la musique* (Paris, 1926).
65. Hans von Wolzogen, *Glaube und Leben* (Berlin, 1908), pp. 157-165.
66. Lissauer, *Die ewigen Pfingsten* (Jena, 1919), pp. 46-51.
67. Lissauer, *Bach: Idyllen und Mythen* (Berlin, 1916).
68. Plattensteiner, *Musikalische Gedichte* (Dresden, 1927) and *Neue Musikalische Gedichte* (Dresden, 1928). He had already devoted a tableau-play to Beethoven: *Beethoven, der grosse Musikant zur Ehre Gottes* (Wien, 1916).
69. Anonymous, *Das Orchester* (Einsiedeln, 1923).
70. Madrid, n. d.

CHAPTER II

1. *Appels d'Orphée*, p. 11. In this connection, see the entire essay, "La musique, vice littéraire," pp. 2-23.
2. Faguet, *L'art de lire* (Paris, 1929), p. 72. An analysis of one of La Fontaine's fables in terms of this "harmony" is given on p. 79 ff.
3. *Sämtliche Werke von Detlev von Liliencron* (Berlin, n. d.), VII, 51-52.
4. Wight Duff, *A Literary History of Rome from the Origins to the Close of the Golden Age* (London, 1925), p. 152, note 3.
5. Verlaine, *Poèmes saturniens*, 1866.
6. Cœuroy, *Appels d'Orphée*, p. 119.
7. *Musikalische Gedichte*, p. 25.

8. John Payne, *New Poems* (London, 1880), pp. 280-283.

9. John Payne, *Intaglios* (London, 1871), p. 59.

10. Ujejski, *Wybór Poezyj* (Kraków, 1924), p. 107. I am indebted to Mr. T. W. Malinowski of Chicago for this translation and for my information as to the rhythmic effects of the original.

11. *The Literary Digest,* Aug. 23, 1930.

12. *Neue Musikalische Gedichte,* p. 51.

13. Sacheverell Sitwell, *The Hundred and One Harlequins* (London, 1922), pp. 22-23.

14. *Neue Musikalische Gedichte,* pp. 51-52.

15. Amy Lowell, *Sword Blades and Poppy Seed* (London, 1914), pp. 155-159.

16. John Murray Gibbon, *Melody and the Lyric from Chaucer to the Cavaliers* (London, 1930), pp. 63-64. For further examples of this practice, see Bruce Pattison, *Music and Poetry of the English Renaissance* (London, 1948), pp. 173-178.

17. Cäsar Flaischlen has a number of "Singlieder" for which he suggests standard tunes. (*Zwischenklänge: Altes und Neues,* Stuttgart, 1921.) One song (p. 89) may be sung to any of five different tunes, or "jede Strophe wechselnd."

18. *The Collected Poems of Edith Sitwell* (London, 1930).

19. *Ibid.*

20. *Ibid.*

21. *Wybór Poezyj,* pp. 106-107.

22. *The Poetical Works of Frances Ridley Havergal* (London, 1884), II, 23-29.

23. *Sounds and Sweet Airs,* pp. 59-67.

24. *Musikalische Gedichte,* pp. 28-30.

25. Bloch, *La nuit kurde* (Paris, 1933), pp. 129, 189-201.

26. First published in 1919. Now most readily accessible in Aiken, *The Divine Pilgrim* (Athens, Ga., 1949), pp. 285-288.

27. Cœuroy, *Musique et littérature,* pp. 68-72.

28. *Ibid.,* p. 71.

29. *Ibid.,* p. 73.

30. Section V, "Iseult at Tintagel."

31. See, for examples, Sacheverell Sitwell, *The Cyder Feast and Other Poems* (London, 1927); Richard Plattensteiner, *Neue musikalische Gedichte* (Leipzig, 1928), pp. 21, 52; Madeleine Merens-Melmer, *Sous la signe de la musique* (Paris, 1926); John Gould Fletcher, *Preludes and Symphonies* (New York, 1930), pp. 50-51.

32. Josef Weinheber, *Hier ist das Wort* (Salzburg, 1947), pp. 31-32, 117-118.

33. Josef Weinheber, *Adel und Untergang* (München, 1943), pp. 37-45.

34. E. H. W. Meyerstein, *Three Sonatas* (privately printed: Bath, 1948), pp. 16-19.

35. R. W. Gilder, *A Book of Music* (N. Y., 1906), "Listening to Music," p. 12.

36. Gabriele d'Annunzio, *L'Orto e la prora* (Verona, 1930), p. 37.

37. *Poetical Works,* II, 23.

38. D'Annunzio, *L'Orto e la prora,* p. 38.

39. *Neue musikalische Gedichte,* pp. 29-31.

40. George Sand, *La coupe, etc.* (Paris, 1876), pp. 261-298.

41. *Blackwood's Edinburgh Magazine,* December, 1849. For a detailed analysis of this literary adaptation of the fugue, see my article, "The Musical Structure of De Quincey's 'Dream Fugue,'" *Musical Quarterly,* XXIV, 341-350. The essential part of this study is reproduced in Chapter XIII of my *Music and Literature.*

42. Schwartz, *In Dreams Begin Responsibilities* (Norfolk, 1938), pp. 91-104.

43. G. H. Conkling, *Afternoons of April* (Boston, 1915), "Symphony of a Mexican Garden," pp. 13-20.

44. Legge, *A Symphony and Other Pieces* (London, 1913), pp. 1-47.

45. Fletcher, *Preludes and Symphonies* (N. Y., 1930).

46. Mary Alice Vialls, *Music Fancies and Other Verses* (Westminster, 1889), pp. 7-8.

47. *Ibid.,* p. 11.

CHAPTER III

1. Weld, "An Experimental Study of Musical Enjoyment," *American Journal of Psychology,* April, 1912.

2. Schoen, *The Beautiful in Music*

(London, 1928), pp. 32-35. Schoen is summarizing Charles S. Myer's *Individual Differences in Listening to Music.*
3. Vernon Lee (pseudonym for Violet Paget), *Music and its Lovers: An Experimental Study of Emotion and Imaginative Responses to Music* (London, 1932).
4. *Ibid.*, Chapter III.
5. Cœuroy, *Appels d'Orphée*, p. 17.
6. *Ibid.*, p. 15.
7. Eduard Hanslick, *Vom Musikalisch-Schönen* (Leipzig, 1922), p. 70.
8. E. W. Naylor, *The Poets and Music* (London, 1928), pp. 18-19.
9. *Ibid*, p. 5, cites a passage from a Galuppi *Sonata in D* to illustrate this line.
10. Stanza xlii.
11. Stanza xci ff.
12. See the Cambridge Edition.
13. Masters, "Beethoven's Ninth Symphony and the King Cobra," *Invisible Landscapes* (N. Y., 1935), pp. 31-45. First published in *The American Mercury*, October, 1932.
14. Henry Van Dyke, *Music and Other Poems* (London, 1904), "Music, an Ode," vii.
15. Jean Richepin, *La mer* (Paris, 1886), p. 194. The notes are listed in this order because the melody opens on *mi,* and *do* is the central point.
16. Maurice Brillant, *Musique sacrée, musique profane* (Paris, 1921), Sérénade pour Pétrouchka," pp. 87-91.
17. R. W. Gilder, *The Fire Divine* (N. Y., 1907), pp. 47-48.
18. *Musikalische Gedichte*, p. 9.
19. *Poems of Sidney Lanier* (N. Y., 1884), pp. 60-70.
20. *The Poems of Alice Meynell* (Lon-

don, 1923), p. 122.
21. *A Book of Music,* p. 55.
22. *La mer,* pp. 194-206.
23. *Sounds and Sweet Airs,* pp. 86-96.
24. "The Eve of St. Agnes," line 57.
25. *Literary Digest,* Jan. 31, 1931.
26. *The Poems of Alice Meynell,* pp. 11-14.
27. *A Book of Music,* p. 39.
28. *Ibid.*, pp. 50-51.
29. Moritz Katz, *Die Schilderung des musikalischen Eindrucks bei Schumann, Hoffmann und Tieck* (Leipzig, 1910), p. 34.
30. Lissauer, *Bach, Idyllen und Mythen,* p. 27. Lissauer uses a similar figure for Beethoven: see *Die Ewigen Pfingsten,* pp. 46-47.
31. *Ibid.*, p. 9.
32. Grace Hazard Conkling, *Witch and Other Poems* (N. Y., 1929).
33. Albert Mérat, *Chansons et madrigaux* (Paris, 1902), p. 77.
34. Ada M. Ingpen, *Music in Poetry and Prose* (London, 1912), pp. 312-313.
35. Werfel, *Die Weltfreund* (Leipzig, 1912), p. 62.
36. S. Sassoon, *Satirical Poems* (1926).
37. *Literary Digest,* Aug. 23, 1930.
38. *New Republic,* June 13, 1928.
39. Will Vesper, *Die Ernte seit Goethe* (Ebenhausen bei München, n. d.), p. 33.
40. *Music and its Lovers,* pp. 359-360.
41. *Sounds and Sweet Airs,* p. 84.
42. *Ibid.*, p. 10.
43. Mérat, *Chansons et madrigaux,* p. 77.
44. *Sounds and Sweet Airs,* p. 87.
45. *Gedichte von Eduard Mörike* (Stuttgart, n. d.), pp. 258-260.
46. Henry Aylett Sampson, *Sonnets and Other Poems* (N. Y., 1920), "Death of Ase," p. 38.

CHAPTER IV

1. *Esprit, saillies, et singularités du P. Castel* (Amsterdam, 1763), pp. 278-347.
2. *Ibid.*, pp. 369-370.
3. Newton, *Optics,* Book I, Part II, Proposition III.
4. For a general history of the problem see Jules Millet, *Audition colorée* (Montpélier, 1892).
5. Erika von Siebold, "Synästhesien in

der englischen Dichtung des 19. Jahrhunderts," *Englische Studien,* 53, 1-157 and 196-334.
6. Erika von Erhardt-Siebold, "Harmony of the Senses in English, French, and German Romanticism," *PMLA*, XLVII, 577-592.
7. *Grillparzers Werke* (Leipzig, 1903), "Stabat Mater," I, 146-147.
8. Erika v. Siebold, *op. cit.*, pp. 19-20.

9. For a general discussion, see Marie-Antoinette Chaix, *La correspondance des arts dans la poésie contemporaine* (Paris, 1919).

10. Baudelaire, *Les fleurs du mal,* IV.

11. Babbitt, *op. cit.,* p. 177.

12. René Ghil, *Traité du verbe* (Paris, 1886), pp. 25-30.

13. See the statistical tables in Millet, *op. cit.,* pp. 52-55.

14. Rimbaud, *Oeuvres complètes* (Paris, 1932), p. 291.

15. Millet, *op. cit.,* pp. 47-48.

16. Ernest Gaubert, "Une explication nouvelle des voyelles d'Arthur Rimbaud," *Mercure de France,* 52, 551-553 (October-December, 1904).

17. Henry Van Dyke, *Music and Other Poems* (London, 1904), "Iris."

18. André Gide, *Two Symphonies* (London, 1931), p. 192.

19. William Gardiner, *The Music of Nature* (London, 1932), p. 188.

20. René Ghil, *op. cit.,* p. 27.

21. Albert Lavignac, *La musique et les musiciens* (Paris, 1895), p. 213.

22. J. L. Hoffmann, quoted by Erika von Siebold, *op. cit.,* p. 51.

23. James Huneker, *Bedouins* (N. Y., 1920), "A Masque of Music," p. 171.

24. Otto Ortmann, "Non-Auditory Effects of Music," in Max Schoen, *The Effects of Music* (N. Y., 1927), p. 251.

25. Alfred Binet, "Le problème de l'audition colorée," *Revue des deux mondes,* October, 1892, p. 599.

26. *Poems by Arthur Upson and George Norton Northrop* (Minneapolis, 1902), XX.

27. E. d'Esterre-Keeling, *The Music of the Poets,* 2nd. ed. (London, 1897), "The Three Fausts," December 11.

28. Erika von Siebold. These are some of the headings under which the examples of synaesthesia from nineteenth-century poetry are grouped.

29. Jules Combarieu, *Les rapports de la musique et de la poésie* (Paris, 1893), Preface, p. xix.

30. Erika von Siebold, *op. cit.,* p. 52.

31. André Suarès, *Musique et poésie* (Paris, 1928), p. 43.

32. "Israfel" (pseudonym for someone who had a sufficient sense of shame to avoid putting his real name to the work), *Musical Fantasies* (London, 1903), p. 11.

33. Katz, *Die Schilderung des musikalischen Eindrucks bei Schumann, Hoffmann und Tieck* (Leipzig, 1910), p. 4.

34. Millet, *op. cit.,* pp. 59-75.

35. Lee, *op. cit.,* p. 440 ff.

36. Percy A. Scholes, *Crotchets: A Few Short Musical Notes* (London, 1924), p. 177.

37. Cowper, *The Task,* VI, 6-18.

38. Ricarda Huch, *Neue Gedichte* (Leipzig, 1907), "Am Klavier," p. 47.

39. *The Works and Life of Walter Savage Landor* (London, 1876), "On Music," VIII, 222.

40. *The Poems of Celia Thaxter* (N. Y., 1898), pp. 184-185.

41. Baker Brownell, in *Poetry: a Magazine of Verse,* March, 1918.

42. Hi Simons, *Ibid.,* February, 1922.

43. Gilder, *A Book of Music,* "Handel's Largo," pp. 30-31.

44. A brief discussion of these borrowings, with illustrations from the original texts, is readily accessible in Robert M. Myers, *Handel's Messiah: A Touchstone of Taste* (N. Y., 1948), pp. 69-72.

45. Hanslick, *Musikalisches und Litterarisches* (Berlin, 1889), "Grillparzer als Musiker."

46. George Sand, *Lettres d'un voyageur* (Paris, 1869), p. 10 and p. 321.

47. *Ibid.,* p. 56.

48. *Music and its Lovers,* pp. 334-338.

CHAPTER V

1. Fanny Green, *Sound Pictures, or, The Beautiful in Music* (London, 1907), p. 7.

2. Lewis Nichols, "Talk with Aaron Copland," N. Y. *Times Book Review* Oct. 19, 1952, p. 47.

3. F. E. Jencken, *Essay on the Poetic Signification of Beethoven's Sonatas* (London, 1871).

4. Edward Macdowell, *Critical and Historical Essays* (N. Y., 1912), pp. 261-273.

5. Harry Porter Weld, "An Experimental Study of Musical Enjoyment,"

American Journal of Psychology, 23, 274-277 (April, 1912).

6. *Ibid.*

7. Mme. E. Quinet, *Ce que dit la musique* (Paris, 1893).

8. Lee, *Music and its Lovers*, p. 327.

9. *Ibid.*

10. P. B. Marston, *A Last Harvest: Lyrics and Sonnets from the Book of Love* (London, 1891), pp. 54-55.

11. R. U. Johnson, *Songs of Liberty and Other Poems* (N. Y., 1897), pp. 20-23.

12. Lee, *op. cit.*, p. 399.

13. Niecks, *Frederick Chopin as a Man and Musician* (London, n. d.), II, 43.

14. One of them, for instance, adds a "beautiful siren." See E. B. Perry, *Descriptive Analyses of Piano Works* (Philadelphia, 1902), pp. 161-167.

15. James Huneker, *Chopin: the Man and his Music* (N. Y., 1905), p. 229.

16. *Poems by Arthur Upson and George Norton Northrop* (Minneapolis, 1902).

17. John Todhunter, *Sounds and Sweet Airs*, pp. 81-85.

18. *The Poetical Works of Mrs. Felicia Hemans* (London, n. d.), pp. 461-463.

19. Richard Wagner, "Beethoven," *Gesammelte Schriften und Dichtungen*, dritte Auflage (Leipzig, 1898), IX, 96-97.

20. Emanuel Geibel, *Gedichte* (Stuttgart, 1884), pp. 10-11. The chorus here is one of the inaccuracies, for at this point only the two solo voices, soprano and alto, are singing.

21. M. J. Estcourt, *Music, the Voice of Harmony in Creation*, p. 102.

CHAPTER VI

1. Schopenhauer, *Schriften über Musik*, p. 135.

2. Lee, *op. cit.*, pp. 383-391.

3. De Quincey, *Confessions of an English Opium-Eater* (London, 1934), p. 265.

4. Weld, *op. cit.*, p. 285.

5. John Payne, *New Poems* (London, 1880), pp. 280-283.

6. Todhunter, *Sounds and Sweet Airs*, p. 54.

7. Wollaston, *The Poets' Symphony* (London, 1913).

8. Christopher Pearse Cranch, *Ariel and Caliban and Other Poems*.

9. Gilder, *A Book of Music*, p. 39.

10. R. Newmarch, *Horae Amoris* (London, 1903), p. 37.

11. R. Newmarch, *Tchaikovsky: his Life and Works* (London, 1900), p. 107.

12. H. Allorge, *Le clavier des harmonies*, pp. 51-52.

13. Nietzsche, *Die Geburt der Tragödie aus dem Geiste der Musik* (Reclam: Leipzig, n. d.), pp. 108-109.

14. Millay, *The Buck in the Snow and Other Poems* (N. Y., 1928), p. 69.

15. Ricarda Huch, *Alte und neue Gedichte* (Leipzig, n. d.), p. 13.

16. H. E. Jakob, *Verse der Lebenden*, 3rd ed. (Berlin, n. d.), p. 140.

17. *Good Housekeeping*, 94, 121 (Jan., 1932).

18. A. Lowell, *Sword Blades and Poppy Seed* (London, 1914), pp. 155-159.

19. Carl Spitteler, *Lachende Wahrheiten* (Leipzig, 1898), pp. 151-156.

20. Allorge, *op. cit.*, p. 128.

21. *Das Orchester* (Einsiedeln, 1923), p. 41.

22. E. Manuel, *Poésies complètes* (Paris, 1899), pp. 348-349.

23. Tolstoi, *The Kreutzer Sonata*, Ch. 23.

24. *Sounds and Sweet Airs*, p. 83.

25. *Ibid.*, pp. 83-84.

26. H. A. Sampson, *Sonnets and Other Poems* (N. Y., 1920), p. 38.

27. Ernst Lissauer, *Gloria Anton Bruckners* (Stuttgart, 1921), p. 14.

28. J. A. Fuller-Maitland, *The Spell of Music* (London, 1926), p. 91.

29. C. Aiken, "Melody in a Restaurant," *Poetry: a Magazine of Verse*, August, 1919.

30. Schopenhauer, *Schriften über Musik*, pp. 146-147.

31. Grove, *Beethoven and his Nine Symphonies* (London, 1896), p. 146.

32. Lee, *op. cit.*, pp. 295-296.

33. Cranch, *Ariel and Caliban and Other Poems*.

CHAPTER VII

1. Plattensteiner, *Neue musikalische Gedichte,* pp. 31-34.
2. Todhunter, *Sounds and Sweet Airs,* pp. 86-96.
3. *The American Mercury,* 27, 129-139 (October, 1932).
4. See L. Hoffmann, *Ein Programm zu Beethovens Neunter Symphonie* (Berlin, 1870). It is interesting to note that Hoffmann interprets the first movement as a representation of chaos before the creation of the world. He says that Goethe's *Faust,* Part II ("Kein Weg! In's Unbetretene" to "Umschwebt von Bildern aller Creatur"), is an excellent motto for the entire first movement, and especially for its conclusion. See also Mme. Edgar Quinet, *op. cit.*
5. Grove, *op. cit.,* p. 354.
6. Ehlert, *Briefe,* p. 14. (Grove's note.)
7. *Neue musikalische Gedichte,* p. 20.
8. Lissauer, *Die ewigen Pfingsten* (Jena, 1919), p. 46.
9. Such interpretation is not unusual. Wagner's conception of a Beethoven quartette as a history of the composer throughout a day has already been mentioned.
10. 2nd. ed. (London, n. d.), pp. 338-339.
11. See p. 116, first excerpt.
12. Grove, *op. cit.,* p. 342.
13. *Ibid.,* p. 352.
14. *Ibid.,* p. 318.
15. *Ibid.,* p. 314.
16. *Ibid.,* p. 355.
17. *Ibid.,* p. 361. This pastoral interpretation of the oboe is a good specimen of Spitteler's orchestral allegory.
18. *Ibid.,* p. 379.
19. Lines 373 and 376. (My italics.)

CHAPTER VIII

1. Gehring, *The Basis of Musical Pleasure* (N. Y., 1910).
2. Benoist-Méchin, *La musique et l'immortalité dans l'œuvre de Marcel Proust* (Paris, 1926), pp. 32-33.
3. *Briefe von Felix Mendelssohn Bartholdy* (Cambridge, 1887), p. 80 (Oct. 15, 1842).
4. *Musikalische Gedichte,* p. 7.
5. *Ibid.,* pp. 45-46.
6. J. Combarieu, *Les rapports de la musique et de la poésie* (Paris, 1893), p. 173, note.
7. Lessing, *Laokoon,* VI.

Select Bibliography

◇

I. MUSIC AND LITERATURE

Ambros, Wilhelm August. *Die Grenzen der Musik und Poesie: eine Studie zur Asthetik der Tonkunst* (Leipzig, 1872). English translation: *The Boundaries of Music and Poetry* (N. Y., 1893).

Baldensperger, Fernand. *La musique dans la littérature contemporaine* (Lyon, 1908).

—————. *Sensibilité musicale et romantisme* (Paris, 1925).

Beattie, James. *Essays on Poetry and Music, as they Affect the Mind*, 3rd ed. (London, 1779).

Benoist-Méchin. *La musique et l'immortalité dans l'œuvre de Marcel Proust* (Paris, 1926).

Benz, Richard. *Die Welt der Dichter und die Musik* (Düsseldorf, 1949).

Boyd, Morrison C. *Elizabethan Music and Musical Criticism* (Philadelphia, 1940).

Brown, Calvin S. *Music and Literature: a Comparison of the Arts* (Athens, Ga., 1948).

Brown, J. *A Dissertation on the Rise, Union, and Power, the Progressions, Separations, and Corruptions of Poetry and Music* (London, 1763).

Cœuroy, André. *Appels d'Orphée: nouvelles études de musique et de littérature comparées* (Paris, 1928).

—————. *Musique et littérature: études de musique et de littérature comparées* (Paris, 1923).

Combarieu, Jules. *Les rapports de la musique et de la poésie, considerées au point de vue de l'expression* (Paris, 1893).

Eliot, T. S. *The Music of Poetry* (Glasgow, 1942).

Evans, Raymond Leslie. *Les romantiques français et la musique* (Paris, 1934).

Faner, Robert D. *Walt Whitman and Opera* (Philadelphia, 1951).

Fuller-Maitland, J. A. "Music and Letters," *Essays and Studies by Members of the English Association*, 17, 44-45.

Gibbon, John Murray. *Melody and the Lyric from Chaucer to the Cavaliers* (London, 1930).

Glöckner, Ernst. *Studien zur romantischen Psychologie der Musik, besonders mit Rücksicht auf die Schriften E. T. A. Hoffmanns* (München, 1909).

Hadow, W. H. *A Comparison of Poetry and Music* (Cambridge, 1926).

—————. *Collected Essays* (London, 1928).

Hanslick, Eduard. *Musikalische Stationen* (Berlin, 1880).

—————. *Musikalisches und Litterarisches* (Berlin, 1889).

Huxley, Aldous. "Music and Poetry," *Texts and Pretexts* (London, 1932), pp. 237-254.

150

Katz, Moritz. *Die Schilderung des musikalischen Eindrucks bei Schumann, Hoffmann und Tieck* (Leipzig, 1910).

Lanier, Sidney. *Music and Poetry* (N. Y., 1898).

Lightwood, James T. *Music and Literature* (London, 1931).

Mallarmé, Stephane. "La musique et les lettres," *Studies in European Literature* (Oxford, 1900), pp. 131-145.

Manganaro, Giovanni L. *Musica e poesia: saggio di critica estetica* (Palermo, 1911).

Martineau, Henri. *Les poètes et la musique* (Alençon, 1923).

Naylor, Edward W. *Shakespeare and Music* (London, 1931).

——————. *The Poets and Music* (London, 1928).

Pattison, Bruce. *Music and Poetry of the English Renaissance* (London, 1948).

Sachs, Curt. *The Commonwealth of Art: Style in the Fine Arts, Music, and the Dance* (N. Y., 1946).

Seseni, Ugo. *Poesia e musica nella latinità cristiana dal III al X secolo* (Torino, 1949).

Spaeth, S. G. *Milton's Knowledge of Music: its Sources and its Significance in his Works* (Weimar, 1913).

Suarès, André. *Musique et poésie* (Paris, 1928).

II. MUSICAL AESTHETICS

Avison, Charles. *An Essay on Musical Expression* (London, 1753).

Busoni, Ferruccio. *Entwurf einer neuen Asthetik der Tonkunst* (Leipzig, n. d.)

Combarieu, Jules. *La musique: ses lois, son évolution* (Paris, 1907).

Elster, Alexander. *Musik und Erotik* (Bonn, 1925).

Fuller-Maitland, J. A. *The Spell of Music: an Attempt to Analyse the Enjoyment of Music* (London, 1926).

Gatz, Felix M. (ed.). *Musik-Aesthetik in ihren Hauptrichtungen* (Stuttgart, 1929).

Gray, Cecil. *Predicaments, or Music and the Future* (London, 1936).

Grove, George. *Beethoven and his Nine Symphonies* (N. Y., 1903).

Gardiner, William. *The Music of Nature* (London, 1832).

Hanslick, Eduard. *Vom Musikalisch-Schönen, ein Beitrag zur Revision der Asthetik der Tonkunst* (Leipzig, 1922).

Haydon, Glen. *On the Meaning of Music* (Washington, D. C., 1948).

Hospers, John. *Meaning and Truth in the Arts* (Chapel Hill, N. C., 1946).

Laprade, Victor de. *Contre la Musique* (Paris, 1881).

Lee, Vernon (pseudonym for Violet Paget). *Music and its Lovers: an Empirical Study of Emotion and Imaginative Responses to Music* (London, 1932).

MacDowell, Edward. *Critical and Historical Essays* (N. Y., 1912).

Niecks, Frederick. *Programme Music in the Last Four Centuries: a Contribution to the History of Musical Expression* (London, 1906).

Schäfke, Rudolf. *Eduard Hanslick und die Musikästhetik* (Leipzig, 1922).

Schering, Arnold. *Das Symbol in der Musik* (Leipzig, 1941).

Schoen, Max. *The Beautiful in Music* (London, 1928).

—————. *The Effects of Music* (N. Y., 1927).

Schopenhauer, A. *Schriften über Musik im Rahmen seiner Asthetik,* edited by Karl Stabenow (Regensburg, 1922).

Sorantin, Erich. *The Problem of Musical Expression* (Nashville, 1932).

Spitteler, Carl. *Lachende Wahrheiten: gesammelte Essays* (Leipzig, 1898).

Weckherlin, J. B. *Nouveau musicana: extraits d'ouvrages rares ou bizarres* (Paris, 1890).

Weingartner, Felix. *Akkorde: gesammelte Aufsätze* (Leipzig, 1912).

Weld, Harry Porter. "An Experimental Study of Musical Enjoyment," *American Journal of Psychology,* April, 1912.

III. Synaesthesia and the Confusion of the Arts

Anschütz, Georg. *Das Farbe-Ton Problem im psychischen Gesamtbereich: Sonderphänomene komplexer optischer Synästhesien* (Halle a. S., 1929).

Babbitt, Irving. *The New Laokoon: an Essay on the Confusion of the Arts* (London, 1910).

Binet, Alfred. "Le problème de l'audition colorée," *Revue des deux mondes,* Oct. 1892, pp. 586-614.

Carol-Bérard, "La couleur en mouvement, décor rationnel de la musique," *Revue musicale,* Aug., 1922, pp. 147-161.

Castel, Louis-Bertrand. *Esprit, saillies, et singularités du P. Castel* (Amsterdam, 1763).

Chaix, Marie-Antoinette. *La correspondance des arts dans la poésie contemporaine: étude psychologique* (Paris, 1919).

Darwin, Erasmus. "The Loves of the Plants," *The Botanic Garden* (London, 1791), Interlude III.

Erhardt-Siebold, Erika von. "Harmony of the Senses in English, German, and French Romanticism," *PMLA,* 47, 577-592 (June, 1932).

Hadow, Sir Henry. *The Place of Music among the Arts* (Oxford, 1933).

Klein, Adrian Bernard. *Colour Music: the Art of Light,* 2nd ed. (London, 1930).

Hoffmann, Johann Leonhard. *Versuch einer Geschichte der malerischen Harmonie überhaupt und der Farbenharmonie insbesondere* (Halle, 1786).

Millet, Jules. *Audition colorée* (Montpellier, 1892).

Rimington, A. W. *Colour-Music: the Art of Mobile Colour* (London, 1912).

Siebold, Erika von. "Synästhesien in der englischen Dichtung des 19. Jahrhunderts: ein ästhetisch-psychologischen Versuch," *Englische Studien,* 53, 1-157 and 196-334.

IV. Anthologies of Literature About Music

Dittberner, Siegfried. *Goldene Worte über Musik und Musiker* (Leipzig, 1923).

Dodsworth, Jessie Eloise. *Musical Moments: Short Selections in Prose and Verse for Music Lovers,* new & enlarged ed. (Chicago, 1893).

Estcourt, Mary Jane. *Music, the Voice of Harmony in Creation* (London, 1857).

Esterre-Keeling, Eleonore d'. *The Music of the Poets: a Musicians' Birthday Book* (London, 1889).

Howard, Esme J. *Music in the Poets: an Anthology* (London, 1927).

Ingpen, Ada M. *Music in Poetry and Prose* (London, 1912).

Kloss, Erich. *Richard Wagner im Liede: Verse deutscher Dichter* (Berlin, 1909).

Koelle, L. L. Carmela. *Music in Song from Chaucer to Tennyson, being a Selection of Extracts Descriptive of the Power, Influences, and Effects of Music* (London, 1883).

Macdougall, Duncan & August. *The Bond of Music: an Anthology* (London, 1906).

Reich, Willi. *Musik in romantischer Schau: Visionen der Dichter* (Basel, 1946).

Sayle, Charles. *In Praise of Music* (London, 1897).

Seebass, Adolf. *Trösterin Musik* (Zürich, 1946).

Wollaston, George Hyde. *The Poets' Symphony, being a Collection of Verses Written by Some of Those Who in Time Past Have Loved Music* (London, 1913).

V. Collections of Poems on Music by Single Authors
(Poems on individual compositions are indicated.)

Allorge, Henri. *Le clavier des harmonies: transcriptions poétiques* (Paris, 1907).
    1. "La tétralogie" (Wagner's "Ring"), pp. 48-50.
    2. "Tristan et Yseult" (Wagner), pp. 51-52.
    3. "Parsifal" (Wagner), pp. 53-54.
    4. Rouget de l'Isle ("La Marseillaise"), pp. 23-25.

Escohotado, Vincente. *La musiquea: poema cómico* (Madrid, n. d.).

Fontenais, André. "Six rondels pour des musiciens," *Revue musicale,* June-July, 1937, pp. 125-128.
    5. (Debussy, "Jardins sous la pluie.")
    6. (Florent Schmitt, "La tragédie de Salomé.")
    7. (Albert Roussel, "Pour un fête de printemps.")
    8. (Ravel, "Le tombeau de Couperin.")
    9. (Dukas, "L'apprenti sorcier."
   10. (Debussy, "L'après-midi d'un faune.")

Gilder, Richard Watson. *A Book of Music* (New York, 1906).
   11. "Listening to Music" (Rubenstein, "Ocean Symphony") p. 12.
   12. "Handel's Largo," pp. 30-31.
   13. "The Pathetic Symphony" (Tschaikowsky), p. 39.

Merens-Melmer, Madeleine. *Sous la signe de la musique* (Paris, 1926).

Miller, Jewell. *Polonaise Militaire: The Life and Work of Frédéric Chopin* (New York, 1936).

14. ("Impromptu," Op. 36), pp. 22-23.
15. ("Polonaise Militaire"), pp. 34-37.
16. ("Scherzo in C# Minor"), p. 64.
17. ("Mazurka in B Flat Minor"), pp. 77-79.
18. (Bach, "Air for the G String"), pp. 121-122.

Orchester, Das (anonymous).   (Einsiedeln, 1923).

Plattensteiner, Richard. *Musikalische Gedichte* (Leipzig, 1927).
19. "Symphonie" (Beethoven's "Fifth"?), pp. 11-12.
20. "Appassionata" (Beethoven), p. 16.
21. "Fünfte Symphonie" (Beethoven), pp. 19-20.
22. "Pastorale" (Beethoven's "Sixth"), pp. 23-26.
23. "Siebente Symphonie" (Beethoven), pp. 28-30.
24. "Der 'Neunten' " (Beethoven), p. 32.
25. "Ein Herbstpoem" (Josef Marx), p. 48.
26. "Vereint" (Finale of Brahms' "First"), p. 49.

Plattensteiner, Richard. *Neue musikalische Gedichte* (Leipzig, 1928).
27. "Der Unvollendeten" (Schubert), p. 7.
28. "Schubert, I. Symphonie," pp. 10-11.
29. "Mozarts Symphonie in D-Dur," pp. 14-15.
30. "Mozart, 'Konzertante' " ("Sinfonie Concertante," K. 364), p. 15.
31. "Mozartvariationen Max Regers," p. 16.
32. "Kreutzer-Sonata" (Beethoven), pp. 20-23.
33. "Beethoven, Opus Nr. 77," p. 23.
34. "Streichquartett Es-Dur" (Beethoven), pp. 24-25.
35. "VIII. Symphonie" (Beethoven), pp. 26-28.
36. "Quartett Opus Nr. 135" (Beethoven), pp. 29-31.
37. "IX. Symphonie" (Beethoven), pp. 31-34.
38. "Schumann 'Ruinen,' " pp. 38-39.
39. "Schumann 'Sternenkranz,' " p. 40.
40. "Zur Phantasie zu Dantes 'Inferno' von Franz Liszt," pp. 40-41.
41. "Brahms, IV. Symphonie," pp. 42-43.
42. "Bruckner, VII. Symphonie," pp. 44-45.
43. "Josef Strauss, 'Mein Lebenslauf ist Lieb und Lust,' " p. 51.
    (Both books of Plattensteiner contain poems on vaguely identified
    works: a Beethoven sonata, a Bruckner symphony, etc.)

Reed, Mary G. *Music and Other Poems* (Boston, 1936).
44. "Fingal's Cave" (Mendelssohn), p. 12.
45. "Handel's Hallelujah Chorus," p. 13.
46. "Rustle of Spring" (Sinding), pp. 14-15.
47. "Clair de Lune" (Debussy), pp. 16-17.

Todhunter, John. *Sounds and Sweet Airs* (London, 1905).
48. "On First Hearing Handel's Messiah," pp. 13-20.
49. "Schubert's Trio in E Flat Major," pp. 34-40.
50. "Schumann's 'Forest Scenes,' " pp. 42-49.
51. "In a Gondola" (Mendelssohn, Op. 19, No. 6), pp. 59-67.
52. "The Wounded Tristram" (Wagner), pp. 69-71.
53. "Tchaikovsky's 'Symphonie Pathétique,' " pp. 76-80.
54. "Dvorák's 'Dumky' Trio," pp. 81-85.

55. "Beethoven's 'Sonata Appassionata,'" pp. 86-96.

Ujejski, Kornel. *Tlumaczenia Szopena*, Biblioteka Pisarzy Polskich, Tom. 43 (Lipsk, 1866). Eight of these poems are more easily accessible in Ujejski, *Wybór Poezyj* (Kraków, 1924).

Z Sonaty (Op. 35).
56. "Marsz pogrzebowy."
57. "Finale."

Preludye (Op. 28).
58. "Wniebowzięcie" (Prelude 7).
59. "Po śmierci" (Prelude 13).
60. "Ostatni bój" (Prelude 20).

Mazurki.
61. "Terkotka" (Op. 30, No. 2).
62. "Na wiosnę" (Op. 33, No. 2).
63. "Zakochana" (Op. 7, No. 2).
64. "Panna mloda" (Op. 7, No. 4).
65. "Kto lepiej?" (Op. 7, No. 5).
66. "Noc straszna" (Op. 6, No. 2).

Vialls, Mary Alice. *Music Fancies and Other Verses* (Westminster, 1899).
67. "Prologue to Mefistofele" (Boito), pp. 1-2.
68. "Adelaide" (Beethoven), p. 4.
69. "Iphigenia in Tauris" (Charles Wood), p. 5.
70. "Prelude to 'Lohengrin'" (Wagner), p. 6.
71. "Overture to 'Tannhäuser" (Wagner), pp. 7-8.
72. "Prize-Song from 'Die Meistersinger'" (Wagner), p. 10.
73. "The Revenge" (C. Villiers Stanford), p. 10.
74. "Nocturne" (Chopin, Op. 37, No. 1), p. 11.
75. "Waltz" (Chopin, Op. 69, No. 1), pp. 13-14.
76. "Barcarolle" (Spohr), p. 16.

VI. SEPARATE POEMS ON MUSICAL COMPOSITIONS

77. Anchusa. "Ravel's Bolero," Chicago *Daily Tribune,* March 9, 1934, p. 10.
78. Annunzio, Gabriele d'. "Ancóra sopra l' 'Erotik'" (Grieg), *L'orto e la prora* (Verona, 1930), p. 37.
79. ——————. "L'apoteosi: L. van Beethoven, op. 26" ("Funeral March"), *Femmine e muse* (Verona, 1929), p. 70.
80. ——————. "Sopra un 'Erotik' di Eduard Grieg," *L'orto e la prora* (Verona, 1930), p. 36.
81. ——————. "Isolda" (Wagner), *Intermezzo* (Rome, 1883).
82. Anonymous. "Haydns Jubeltag" ("The Creation"), *Neue Musik-Zeitung,* V, Nr. 6, 3. Beilage (1884).
83. ——————. *An Ode to Mr. Handel* ("Messiah") (London, 1745).
84. ——————. "On George Frederick Handel, Esq. . . ." ("Messiah"), *Daily Advertiser,* April 17, 1759.
85. ——————. *The Woman of Taste . . .* (Handel, "Esther") (London, 1733).
86. ——————. "Wrote Extempore by a Gentleman, on Reading *the Universal Spectator,* on Mr. Handel's New Oratorio [*Messiah*]," *Daily Advertiser,* March 31, 1743.

87. Banville, Théodore de. "La dernière pensée de Weber" (H. Cramer), *Oeuvres de Théodore de Banville* (Paris, 1889), p. 86.

88. Baring, Maurice. "Tristan and Iseult" (Wagner), *Collected Poems* (London, 1925), p. 32.

89. Beeching, H. C. "Polonaise" (Chopin, Op. 40, No. 2), *In a Garden and Other Poems* (New York, 1895).

90. Blunden, Edmund. "A Quartet ('The Mikado' at Cambridge)," *Poems, 1914-1930* (London, 1930), pp. 285-286.

91. Bowe, Augustine. "Dies Irae," *Poetry: a Magazine of Verse,* LVII, 250-251 (January, 1941).

92. Brillant, Maurice. "Sérénade pour Pétrouchka," *Musique sacrée, musique profane* (Paris, 1921), pp. 87-91.

93. Brown, C. S. "On Handel's 'Messiah,'" *American Mercury,* XXVI, 39-40 (May, 1932).

94. Brown, T. E. "To E. M. O." (Bach, Organ Chorale on "Herzlich thut mich verlangen"), Wollaston (Sec. IV), No. 40.

95. Brownell, Baker. "Taps," *Poetry: a Magazine of Verse,* March, 1918.

96. Browning, Robert. "Parleyings with Charles Avison" (Avison's "Grand March") *Complete Poetic and Dramatic Works* (New York, 1895), pp. 974-979.

97. —————. "Fifine at the Fair" (Schumann, "Carnival"), *Ibid.,* pp. 701-736.

98. Bull, Lucy C. "The Fifth Symphony" (Beethoven), Dodsworth Sec. IV), pp. 142-143.

99. Bunner, H. C. "Schumann's Kinder-Scenen," Dodsworth (Sec. IV), p. 81.

100. Carrington, Mary Coles. "Danse Macabre (Camille Saint-Saëns, Op. 40), *Literary Digest,* Jan. 31, 1931.

101. Cone, Helen Gray. "Bach's St. Matthew Passion Music," Dodsworth (Sec. IV), p. 61.

102. —————. "A Nocturne of Rubenstein (Op. 69)," *Ibid.,* pp. 70-72.

103. Conkling, Grace Hazard. "Brahms — No. 2 in D Major — Op. 73," *Flying Fish: a Book of Songs and Sonnets* (New York, 1926), p. 111.

104. —————. "Fire Dance" (De Falla, "El amor brujo"), *Witch and Other Poems* (New York, 1929).

105. —————. "Haydn — Opus 77 — No. 1," *Ibid.,* p. 64.

106. —————. " 'Nuit d'Étoiles': Claude Debussy," *Wilderness Songs* (New York, 1920), p. 98.

107. —————. " 'Reflets dans l'Eau': Claude Debussy," *Ibid.,* p. 99.

108. Coppée, François. "Adagio" (Beethoven, Op. 101), *Oeuvres complètes* (Paris, n. d.), I, 8-9.

109. Cowper, William. (Handel, "Messiah"), *The Task,* VI, 631-657.

110. Cranch, Christopher Pearse. "Beethoven's Fifth Symphony," *Ariel and Caliban and Other Poems* (New York, 1887).

111. Cummins, P. D. "Pavane for a Dead Infanta" (Ravel), *The Defeated* (London, 1947), p. 34.

112. Dahn, Felix. "Zur 'Träumerei' von Schumann," *Gedichte von Felix Dahn: zweite Sammlung* (Stuttgart, 1873), pp. 379-380.

113. Dehmel, Richard. "Der tote Ton" (a translation of Ujejski's "Marsz pogrzebowy": see Bibliography V), *Gesammelte Werke* (Berlin, 1907), II, 50-56.

114. Dobell, Bertram. "Bach's Second Concerto" (Brandenburg), *A Century of Sonnets* (London, 1910), p. 94.

115. Dohm, Ernst. "Die Meistersinger von Nürnberg" (Wagner), Kloss (Sec. IV), p. 16.

116. —————. "Der Nibelungen Freud und Sieg" (Wagner), *Ibid.*, pp. 12-13.

117. Ellis, Havelock. "The Unfinished Symphony" (Schubert), *Sonnets, with Folk Songs from the Spanish* (New York, 1925), p. 43.

118. Erasmus, Th. "Beethovens Pastoralsymphonie: Paraphrase," *Neue Musik-Zeitung*, VII, Nr. 11, 3. Beilage (1886).

119. Evans, M. A. B. "The Moonlight Sonata," *The Moonlight Sonata and Other Verses* (New York, 1910), pp. 1-7.

120. —————. "Nocturne" (Chopin No. 2), *Ibid.*, p. 39.

121. Feuchtersleben, Ernst von. "Die Zauberflöte" (Mozart), Seebass Sec. IV), p. 26.

122. Foster, Edna A. "Nocturne, Op. 37 — Chopin," Dodsworth (Sec. IV), p. 176.

123. Findeisen, Kurt Arnold. *Robert Schumanns Kinderszenen auf heimatlichem Grund gelegt: eine Dichtung* (Dresden, 1921).

124. Friederich, Paul. *Karneval: heitere Dichtungen zu Robert Schumanns Kompositionen* (Berlin, 1913).

125. Gautier, Théophile. "Variations sur le Carnaval de Venise," *Emaux et camées* (Paris, 1923), pp. 21-32.

126. Gerstenberg, H. W. von. "Hamlet" (a piano Fantasia of C. P. E. Bach), C. F. Cramer, *Flora* (Kiel, 1787).

127. —————. "Socrates" (the same Fantasia as the preceding item), *Ibid.*

128. Geibel, Emanuel. "Pergolesi" ("Stabat Mater"), *Gedichte von Emanuel Geibel* (Stuttgart, 1884), pp. 10-11.

129. Gilder, Richard Watson. "Music in Moonlight" (Schumann, "Mondnacht"), *The Fire Divine* (New York, 1907), pp. 47-48.

130. Godoy, Armand. *Le Carnaval de Schumann* (Paris, 1927).

131. —————. A poem on Beethoven's "Kreutzer Sonata," *Triste et tendre* (Paris, 1927).

132. Graves, C. L. "Mélodie du siècle" (Richard Strauss, "Elektra"), *The Brain of the Nation and Other Poems* (London, 1912), pp. 99-101.

133. —————. "To Engelbert Humperdinck" (Hänsel und Gretel"), *War's Surprises and Other Verses* (London, 1917), pp. 72-74.

134. Gregh, Fernand. "Carnaval: variations sur le Carnaval de Schumann (Op. 9)," *La chaine éternelle* (Paris, 1910), pp. 180-250.

135. Griepenkerl, Wolfgang Robert. Sonnet on the Adagio of Beethoven's "Sonata in C♯ Minor," from the novel *Das Musikfest*. Quoted in *Zeitschrift für Musikwissenschaft*, II, 368.

136. Grillparzer, Franz. "Beethovens neunte Symphonie," *Gesammelte Werke* (Berlin, n. d.), IV.

137. ——————. "Klara Wieck und Beethoven" ("F Minor Sonata"), *Ibid.*

138. ——————. "Paganini" ("Adagio and Rondo on the G String"), *Ibid.*

139. ——————. "Stabat Mater" (Rossini), *Ibid.*

140. ——————. "Zu Beethovens Egmont-Musik," *Ibid.*

141. Gutiérrez Nájera, Manuel. "La Serenata de Schubert," *Poesías de Manuel Gutiérrez Nájera* (Paris, 1912), II, 121-123.

142. Havergal, Frances Ridley. "The Moonlight Sonata" (Beethoven), *Poetical Works* (London, 1884), II, 14-31.

143. ——————. "Threefold Praise" (Haydn, "The Creation"; Mendelssohn, "Elijah"; Handel, "Messiah"), *Ibid.*, I, 11-19.

144. Hemans, Felicia. "Mozart's Requiem," *Poetical Works* (London, n. d.), pp. 461-463.

145. Hitz, Luise. "Parsifal" (Wagner), Kloss (Sec. IV), pp. 26-27.

146. Hollowell, Grace Baer. "Das Rheingold" (Wagner), *Poetry: a Magazine of Verse*, LVII, 240-241.

147. Humes, Jessie Neal. "The Clarinettist Plays" (Debussy, "The Little Shepherd"), *Washington Poets* (New York, 1932), p. 106.

148. John, Edmund. "The Little Shepherd" (Debussy), *The Wind in the Temple* (London, 1915), pp. 32-33.

149. Johnson, Robert Underwood. "A Chopin Fantasy" ("Prelude 15"), *Songs of Liberty and Other Poems* (New York, 1897), pp. 20-23.

150. Josky, Felix. *Gedichte zu den Kinderscenen Robert Schumanns* (Berlin, 1913).

151. König, Eberhard. *Ein Heldenleben* (R. Strauss) (Leipzig, n. d.).

152. Körner, Theodor. "Nach der Aufführung von Händels Alexanderfest in Wien," *Sämmtliche Werke* (Leipzig, n. d.), pp. 138-140.

153. Laird, William. "Träumerei at Ostendorff's" (Schumann), *Poetry: a Magazine of Verse*, Sept., 1914.

154. Langhorne, John. *The Tears of Music: a Poem to the Memory of Mr. Handel* (various works) (London, 1760).

155. Levy, Amy. "Sinfonia Eroica" (Beethoven), Ingpen (Sec. IV), pp. 312-313.

156. Liliencron, Detlev von. "Ballade in G-moll" (Chopin), *Der Haidegänger und andere Gedichte* (Leipzig, n. d.), pp. 92-93.

157. Lissauer, Ernst. "Mit dem Adagio aus dem Streichquintett," *Gloria Anton Bruckners* (Stuttgart, 1921), p. 14.

158. ——————. "Trost des 'Deutschen Requiems'" (Brahms), *Der inwendige Weg* (Jena, 1920), p. 53.

159. Lomtano, Franziska. "Beethovens Sonate Opus 10, F dur," *Neue Musik-Zeitung*, I, Nr. 7 (1880).

160. ——————. "Poetische Erklärung von Beethoven's Sonate E moll op. 90," *Ibid.*, I, Nr. 17 (1880).

161. ——————. "Sonate Opus 53, C dur" (Beethoven), *Ibid.*, I, Nr. 11 (1880).

162. Lowell, Amy. "Stravinsky's Three Pieces 'Grotesques' for String Quartet," *Men, Women, and Ghosts* (Boston, n. d.), pp. 342-347.

163. Lydgate, John. "Incipit de Musica" ("Ut queant laxis"), Estcourt (Sec. IV), pp. 18-20.

164. Malone, Walter. "The Mendelssohn Wedding March," *Songs of Dusk and Dawn* (1894), pp. 54-56.

165. Manuel, Eugène. "Songe d'une nuit d'été" (Mendelssohn), *Poésies complètes* (Paris, 1899), pp. 211-212.

166. Marston, Philip Bourke. "The River" (Chopin, "Prelude 15"), *A Last Harvest: Lyrics and Sonnets from the Book of Love* (London, 1891), pp. 54-55.

167. Masters, Edgar Lee. "Beethoven's Ninth Symphony and the King Cobra," *Invisible Landscapes* (New York, 1935), pp. 31-45.

168. Mérat, Albert. "Camées parisiens" (various musical works in sonnets to singers and actresses), *Chansons et madrigaux* (Paris, 1902).

169. —————. "Souvenir d'Orphée" (Gluck), *Vers oubliés* (Paris, 1902), p. 78.

170. Merrill, Stuart. "La chevauchée des Walkyries" (Wagner), *Poèmes* (1887-1897) (Paris, 1897), p. 87.

171. —————. "Lohengrin," *Ibid.*, p. 85.

172. —————. "Parsifal," *Ibid.*, p. 86.

173. Meynell, Alice. "The Marriage of True Minds" (Bach-Gounod "Ave Maria"), *The Poems of Alice Meynell* (London, 1923), p. 122.

174. —————. "Sœur Monique" (Couperin), *Ibid.*, pp. 11-14.

175. Michaeli, Otto. "Zu Schumanns Klavierstück 'Einsame Blumen' (Waldscenen, Op. 82, Nr. 3)," *Neue Musik-Zeitung*, XIII, 413.

176. Miller, Jewell. "Mendicant Music" (De Capua, "O sole mio"), Mountain Water (North Montpelier, Vt., 1938), pp. 50-51.

177. —————. "The Pines of Rome" (Respighi), *Ibid.*, pp. 55-59.

178. —————. "Valse Triste" (Sibelius), *Ibid.*, p. 93.

179. Morgenstern, Christian. "Zu Beethovens Appassionata," Seebass (Sec. IV), p. 69.

180. Nathan, Robert. "At the Symphony (*César Franck, D Minor*)," Untermeyer, *Modern American Poetry*, 5th revised ed. (New York, n. d.), p. 523.

181. Neumann, Alfred. "J. S. Bach: Suite Nr. 3 in C-Dur," H. E. Jakob, *Verse der Lebenden: deutsche Lyrik seit 1910*, 3rd ed. (Berlin, n. d.), p. 140.

182. Newmarch, Rosa. "The Symphony" (Tschaikowsky, "Pathétique"), *Horae Amoris* (London, 1903), p. 37.

183. Northrop, George Norton. "Beethoven, Op. 31, No. 3, Menuetto," *Poems by Arthur Upson and George Norton Northrop* (Minneapolis, 1902), IV.

184. —————. "Grieg's 'Einsamer Wanderer,' " *Ibid.*, III.

185. Parmenter, Catherine. "The Blue Danube" (J. Strauss), *Literary Digest*, Aug. 23, 1910.

186. —————. "On Hearing Schubert's 'Unfinished Symphony,' " *Good Housekeeping*, 94, 121 (Jan., 1932).

187. Payne, John. "In Armida's Garden" (Gluck, "Armida," II, iii, Introduction and Aria), *Songs of Life and Death* (London, 1872), pp. 22-31.

188. —————. "Love's Autumn" (John Field, "Nocturne in D Minor"), *New Poems* (London, 1880), pp. 280-283.
189. —————. "Bride Night" (Wagner, "Tristan," II, ii), *Intaglios* (London, 1871), p. 59.
190. Perry, Edward B. "Fantasie Impromptu" (Chopin), *Descriptive Analyses of Piano Works* (Philadelphia, n. d.), *p.* 151.
191. —————. "Funeral March" (Chopin), *Stories of Standard Teaching Pieces* (Philadelphia, 1910).
192. —————. "D'Albert: Mélodie," *Ibid.*
193. Pierce, Edith Lovejoy. "Beethoven's Ninth Symphony in Wartime," *In This our Day* (New York, 1944).
194. Richepin, Jean. "Les trois matelots de Groix," *La mer* (Paris, 1886), pp. 194-206.
195. Pousette-Dart, Flora Louise. "Beethoven, Opus 111," *I Saw Time Open* (New York, 1947), pp. 81-82.
196. Ritter, Alexander. "Tod und Kerklärung" (R. Strauss), in orchestra score (München, 1904), p. 2.
197. Rollinat, Maurice. "Marches funèbres" (Beethoven and Chopin), *Les névroses* (Paris, 1889).
198. Sampson, Henry Aylett. "Death of Ase" (Grieg), *Sonnets and Other Poems* (New York, 1920), p. 38.
199. Sampson, Martin Wright. "Flonzaley (Beethoven, op. 127, adagio)," *Voices of the Forest* (Ithaca, N. Y., 1933), p. 41.
200. Sassoon, Siegfried. "Concert Interpretation" (Stravinsky, "Le sacre due printemps"), *Satirical Poems* (London, 1926).
201. —————. "Hommage à Mendelssohn" ("Prelude in A Flat"), *Ibid.*
202. —————. "Sheldonian Soliloquy (During Bach's B Minor Mass)," *Ibid.*
203. Schwartz, Delmore. "Coriolanus and his Mother" (Beethoven, Overture to "Coriolanus"), *In Dreams Begin Responsibilities* (Norfolk, Conn., 1938), p. 33.
204. Scott, William Bell. "Music" (Handel, "Dead March" from "Saul"), *A Poet's Harvest Home* (London, 1893), p. 48.
205. Scruggs, Anderson M. "First Symphony: Johannes Brahms," *What Shall the Heart Remember?* (Athens, Ga., 1951), p. 26.
206. Sewell, W. "Weber's Last Waltz" (H. Cramer), Estcourt (Sec. IV), p. 102.
207. Simons, Hi. "Taps," *Poetry: a Magazine of Verse*, 19, 258.
208. Sitwell, Sacheverell. "Valse Estudiantina" (Waldteufel), *The Hundred and One Harlequins* (London, 1922), pp. 22-23.
209. Strauss, David Friederich. "Händel" ("Messiah"), Seebass (Sec. IV), p. 25.
210. Stuart, Morna. "Pastoral Invocation in Noon" (Franck, "Pastorale"), *Music and Letters*, 18, 239.
211. Swinburne, Algernon Charles. "'Two Preludes'" (Wagner, "Lohengrin" and "Tristan"), *Collected Poetical Works* (New York, n. d.), II, 551-552.
212. Thaxter, Celia. "Schumann's Sonata in A Minor," *The Poems of Celia Thaxter* (New York, 1898), pp. 184-185.

213. Tieck, Ludwig. "Pergolesi" ("Stabat Mater"), *Sämmtliche Werke* (Wien, 1818), XIII, 213-220.

214. Upson, Arthur. "A Motive out of Lohengrin" (Wagner), *The City, a Poem-Drama, and Other Poems* (London, 1905), p. 123.

215. ——————. "Quatrains of Seven Singing Ladies" (several operas), *Poems by Arthur Upson and George Norton Northrop* (Minneapolis, 1902), XX.

216. Verlaine, Paul. "Parsifal" (Wagner), *Revue wagnérienne*, Jan., 1886, p. 336.

217. Vivaldi, Antonio (?). "La primavera," "L'estate," "L'autunno," "L'inverno" (four sonnets containing the programs of Vivaldi's four concertos of the same titles), *Il cimento dell' armonia e dell' invenzione* (Amsterdam, 1720).

218. Watts-Dunton, Theodore. "The Three Fausts" (Berlioz, Gounod, Schumann), d'Esterre-Keeling (Sec. IV), Dec. 11.

219. Weigand, Wilhelm. ("Gigue" of Bach's "First Partita"), quoted in André Pirro, *Bach: Sein Leben und seine Werke* (Berlin, 1919), p. 177.

220. Werfel, Franz. "Konzert einer Klavierlehrerin" (Chopin, "Funeral March"), *Der Weltfreund* (Leipzig, 1912), p. 62.

221. Wheelock, John Hall. "Christmas Eve" (Bach's "Air for the G String), *Poems*, 1911-1936 (New York, 1936, pp. 238-239.

222. ——————. "The Moonlight Sonata" (Beethoven), *Ibid.*, pp. 122-127.

223. ——————. "The Ninth Symphony" (Beethoven), *Ibid.*, p. 110.

224. ——————. "Tchaikovsky: Fifth Symphony," *The Black Panther: a Book of Poems* (New York, 1922), p. 35.

225. Whyte, Laurence. "On Mr. Handel's Performance of his Oratorio, call'd the *Messiah* . . . ," *Faulkner's Journal*, April 20, 1742.

226. Wieland, Christoph Martin. "Haydns Schöpfung," Seebass (Sec. IV), p. 26.

227. Wolfe, Humbert. "August: Après-Midi d'un Faune" (Debussy), *Snow*, (London, 1931), p. 24.

228. ——————. "The Moonlight Sonata" (Beethoven), *The Unknown Goddess* (London, 1925), pp. 59-60.

229. Wolzogen, Hans von. "Die Sieben Werke" (Wagner's seven principal works, the "Ring" being considered as one), *Glaube und Leben* (Berlin, 1908), pp. 157-165.

230. Wyzéwa, Téodor de. "Siegfried-Idyll" (Wagner), *Revue wagnérienne*, Jan., 1886, p. 341.

231. Young, Stark. "To Chopin: His Prelude in C Minor," *The Blind Man at the Window and Other Poems* (New York, 1906), pp. 35-37.

Addenda

"Les œuvres de Richard Wagner" (sonnets), *Revue wagnérienne*, II, 371-379 (Jan., 1887):

232. Jean Richepin, "Le hollandais volant," p. 371.

233. Amédée Pigeon, "Tannhaeuser," p. 272.

234. Jean Ajalbert, "Lohengrin," p. 373.

235. Gabriel Mourey, "Tristan et Isolde," p. 374.

Composer - Index to the Poems of Sections V and VI

◇

(Anonymous works are listed by title. References are to numbers in "Select Bibliography.")

d'Albert, 192.
Avison, Charles, 96.

Bach, C. P. E., 128, 129.
Bach, J. S., 18, 94, 101, 114, 173, 181, 202, 219, 221.
Beethoven, 19-24, 32-37, 55, 68, 79, 98, 108, 110, 118, 119, 127, 135-137, 140, 142, 155, 159-161, 167, 179, 183, 193, 195, 197, 199, 203, 222, 223, 228.
Berlioz, 218.
Bizet, 215.
Boito, 67.
Brahms, 26, 41, 103, 158, 205.
Bruckner, 42, 157.

"Carnival of Venice," 125.
Chopin, 14-17, 56-66, 74, 75, 89, 113, 120, 122, 149, 156, 166, 190, 191, 197, 220, 231.
Couperin, 174.
Cramer, H., 87, 206.

Debussy, 5, 10, 47, 106, 107, 147, 148, 227.
De Capua, 176.
De Falla, 104.
Delibes, 168.
Dukas, 9.
Dvorák, 54.

Field, John, 188.
Franck, 180, 210.

Gluck, 169, 187.
Gounod, 173, 218.
Grieg, 78, 80, 184, 198.

Handel, 12, 45, 48, 83-86, 93, 109, 143, 152, 154, 204, 209, 225.
Haydn, 82, 105, 143, 226.
Humperdinck, 133.

Liszt, 40.

Marx, Josef, 25.

Mendelssohn, 44, 51, 143, 164, 165, 201.
Meyerbeer, 168.
Mozart, 29, 30, (31), 121, 144.

Paganini, 138.
Pergolesi, 130, 213.

Ravel, 8, 77, 111.
Reger, 31.
Respighi, 177.
Rossini, 139.
Rouget de Lisle, 4.
Roussel, 7.
Rubenstein, 11, 102.

Saint-Saëns, 100.
Schmitt, Florent, 6.
Schubert, 27, 28, 49, 117, 141, 186.
Schumann, 38, 39, 50, 97, 99, 112, 123, 124, 126, 131, 134, 150, 153, 175, 212, 218.
Sibelius, 178.
Sinding, 46.
Spohr, 76.
Stanford, C. V., 73.
Strauss, Johann, 185.
Strauss, Josef, 43.
Strauss, Richard, 132, 151, 196.
Stravinsky, 92, 162, 200.
Sullivan, A., 90.

"Taps" (bugle call), 95, 207.
Thomas of Celano (?), 91.
"Trois matelots de Groix," 194.
Tschaikowsky, 13, 53, 182, 224.

"Ut queant laxis," 163.

Verdi, 215.
Vivaldi, 217.

Wagner, 1, 2, 3, 52, 70-72, 81, 88, 115, 116, 145, 146, 170-172, 189, 211, 214, 215, 215, 229, 230, 232-239.
Waldteufel, 208.
Wood, Charles, 69.

Index